MW01675570

Early History of Irish Crochet Lace

Barbara Ballantyne

Early History of Irish Crochet Lace

Published in Australia by Barbara Ballantyne
bjballantyne@ozemail.com.au
www.crochethistory.com
PO Box 435 Drummoyne 1470 NSW Australia

© Barbara Ballantyne 2007

This book is copyright. Apart from exceptions under the Copyright Act, no part may be reproduced, stored in a retrieval system, or transmitted in any form or by any means, electronic, mechanical, photocopying, recording or otherwise without prior written permission. The copyright for the illustrations resides with organization or individual in the attribution below the image. All enquiries should be directed to the author.

National Library of Australia
Cataloguing-in-Publication data

Ballantyne, Barbara
Early History of Irish Crochet Lace.

ISBN 978-0-9580235-2-8 (pbk.)

1. Irish crochet lace. 2. Crocheting – Ireland – History. 3. Lace and lace making – Ireland – History –. I Title.

746.209415

The front cover shows part of a collar, B819 and the back cover a cuff, B687, both from the author's collection.

Set in Garamond Pro 11pt
Typeset, printed and bound in Australia by Ligare Pty Ltd, 138 Bonds Rd., Riverwood, NSW, 2210, Australia.
Cover Design: Henry Welch

CONTENTS

Part II
Revival of the Irish lace Industry

Appendices

Foreword

Barbara Ballantyne has done huge research on the history of Irish crochet, its patrons, stitches, makers and designers as well as giving a very detailed overall-picture of the industry in Ireland.

She has broken new ground in her research on crochet making in the Cork area and provides information which was not previously known about the early years of the industry in the south of Ireland.

She is to be congratulated for her fine reproductions of the older pieces and for the large amount of information she has gathered about Eleonore Riego de la Branchardière.

This woman claimed to have 'invented Irish crochet' but Barbara has restored the credit for creating and developing this lace to the women of Ireland. Mlle Riego and the many other English crochet lace designers of the period made only a very small contribution to Irish crochet lace.

Apart from the information about the technique of Irish crochet, this book shows its economic importance from the era of the Great Famine of the late eighteen forties for many years afterwards. I hope Barbara will continue writing about the .later periods not covered in this book

Nellie Ó Cléirigh
38 Templemore Avenue
Rathgar
Dublin 6
Ireland
10 September 2007

PREFACE

Several years ago I became curious about the Irish crochet lace in the books of Mary Card and in Australian museums. Some of it was very beautiful. Quite often it was different to the designs in overseas books, probably because Mary's work was based on the extensive range of pieces that came to her when she refurbished Irish crochet early in the twentieth century.

The history also caught my interest. The early books tell of the vital role of the nuns, the wives of clergymen and other benevolent women in developing Irish crochet as an attractive lace and an important source of income from the time of the famine. Yet the later books say that Mlle Riego de la Branchardière, a talented and prolific English needlework designer, had 'invented' Irish crochet, without presenting any evidence.

My research took me overseas, to museums, libraries, convents, archives and private collections, in Ireland, London, the USA and France. I found a surprising amount of information about the lace and its early history in old books and official records.

This book tells the stories of the people and places where Irish crochet was worked during the latter part of the 1800s. It also shows what some of the early Irish crochet looked like and traces how it developed from copying other laces, to an art form in its own right.

I have also written a companion book, *Mademoiselle Riego and Irish Crochet Lace,* which looks at the work of Mlle Riego and other English designers of the period to see whether they influenced Irish crochet. It has an unexpected ending.

If your main interest is Irish crochet, I suggest you begin with this book. If your outlook is broader, you may prefer to read the one about Mlle Riego first. Whichever one you chose, the extensive illustrations make it easy to follow the delightful stories.

Acknowledgments

I would like to thank the many people who helped in the preparation of this book.

I particularly appreciated the assistance and hospitality of the remarkable Irish lace historian Nellie Ó Cléirigh, who added significantly to this book. She gave me access to her remarkable library and records. We discussed my findings while I was in Ireland and later in correspondence as I sent my manuscripts back to her.

I am grateful to the County Armagh Museum, the Cork Municipal Museum, the National Museum of Ireland, the Ulster Folk and Transport Museum, Holywood, the Victoria & Albert Museum, the Embroiderers Guilds of New South Wales and Western Australia, the Australian Lace Guild (NSW) Branch, Mary Aikenhead Heritage Centre and Jeanette Moles for giving me access to their Irish crochet lace collections and in some instances for supplying images for use in this book.

The many libraries I used were of great assistance. These included the British Library, the National Art Library of the Victoria & Albert Museum, the National Library of Ireland, the State Library of New South Wales, the State Library of Victoria also the libraries of the Royal Dublin Society, University of Cork, University College Dublin (the O'Kelley Collection, Special Collections), Trinity College Dublin, the Museum of Applied Arts & Science Ultimo (Powerhouse Museum), the Embroiderers' Guild of New South Wales and the Society of Australian Genealogists. Rhonda Henderson provided part of W. Carter's Royal Exhibition Knitting, Netting and Crochet Book. Many of these libraries gave permission for use of images from their collections. Sybil Harland also assisted with literature and showed me her collection of Irish crochet lace.

I gratefully acknowledge use of documents from the Commissioner of Charitable Donations and Bequests, Dublin and the Cork City & County Archives.

Terry Eakin carried out much of the genealogical research, advised on Irish matters and gave me access to his library. Joy Hargans, Dr. Christine Johnson, Coralie Lewin, Jill Monro and Lindie Ward read the manuscript. Anne Savage provided editorial assistance. Bruce Welch of Ligare gave prepress guidance. Wendy Williams made the line drawings of the crochet stitches.

I would like to thank Kathie Earle and Máire Treanor for their help and hospitality. Veronica Stuart assisted also.

My discussions with Rosemary Shepherd have been particularly valuable.

Introduction to Irish Crochet Techniques

A little basic knowledge of the structure and techniques of Irish crochet will enable you to follow the different styles of the lace.

Irish crochet, like all forms of crochet, is based on a loop, used in various ways as shown in the line drawings:

The chain is the simplest stitch:

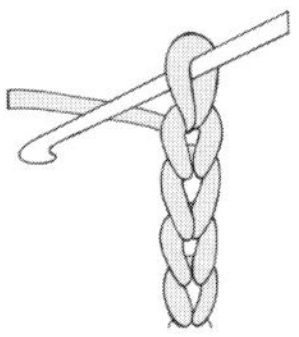

A simple extension is the double crochet (single crochet in the USA) which can give the same effect as the simple buttonhole stitch used to make needle lace:

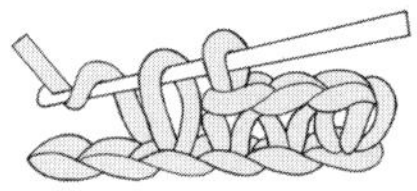

A taller stitch with a twist is the treble (double crochet in the USA):

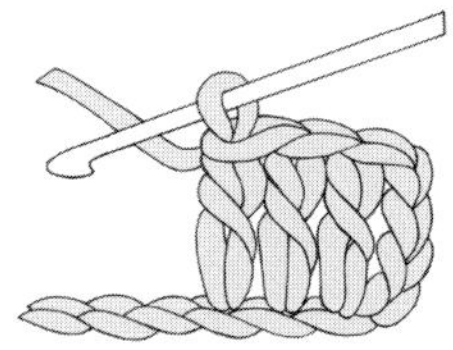

These examples all show the little arrows or chevrons which allow you to distinguish crochet from needle lace.

Irish crochet added some specialized techniques to these basic stitches:

The first was the way of joining the pieces which make up the lace. As with the needle laces, motifs were worked separately, arranged in a design on a foundation of either fabric or stiff paper and tacked in place. The background or ground was then worked between the motifs as in the partly completed piece presented here.

Motifs sewn onto cloth foundation

Another new technique was crocheting over several thicknesses of thread or cord to make the motif more robust and less likely to distort when the ground was added. In the hands of an expert flowers and leaves could be given a more artistic shape and raised effects contributed to the texture.

Crocheting over cord wound in a circle produced padded rings which often formed the centre of motifs.

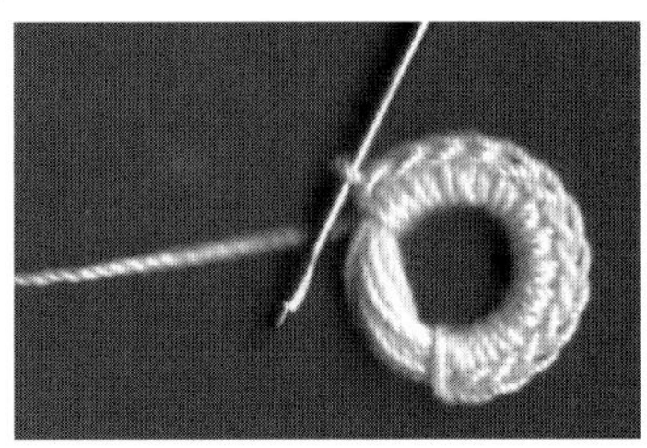

A raised and almost solid disc was produced when the crocheting continued for many rounds, as shown in the lace on the next page, just in from the edges.

The motifs were often in the form of flowers, fruit and leaves, including shamrocks; some were in grotesque shapes.

The ground was usually of fine loops ornamented with small projections (picots) along the bars.

The finished pieces were commonly edged with firm loops covered with double crochet and picots.

Some designs featured Clones knots which are shown as the tiny spheres along the bars in the ground around the motif presented below. This padded ring has the centre filled with a needle lace flower. Crochet fillings also appear later in the book[1].

The Clones knot is an unusual stitch developed by the crocheters at Clones.

It was worked over a length of chain by alternately picking up the thread at the front of the chain, then the back and repeating this many times before drawing the loop on the hook through all the loops over the chain and finishing with a double crochet.

It required considerable skill and practice but was worthwhile as it produced a very rich effect, not only when used in the ground as seen above but also on the surface of motifs and occasionally along the edge.

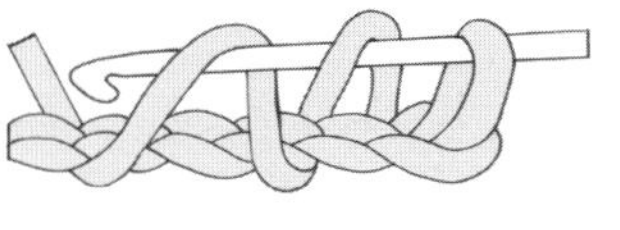

Shamrocks and raised roses were combined with other motifs in the early work where the ground was added at the discretion of the worker.

Then towards the end of the nineteenth century they were used in a different way, worked to an almost set pattern, surrounded by rows of picot loops and shells. These decorative medallions, which were often square, were joined in the working of the last row to make a very wide range of articles and trimmings. This dainty style was eminently suited to the showy Edwardian fashions and became very popular.

Square Medallions[2]

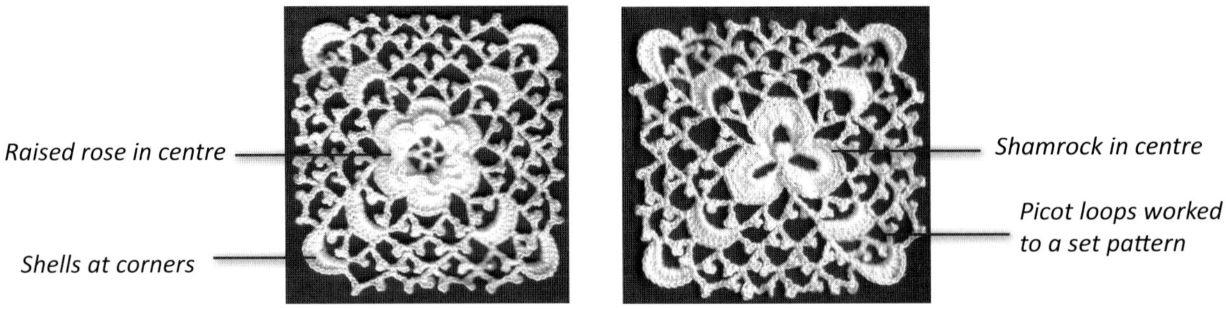

Part I

Beginnings

CHAPTER 1

The First Forty Years

Lacemaking was the salvation of many Irish families in the mid-nineteenth century when a new disease killed the potatoes on which most of the Irish depended. The Great Irish Famine (1845–52) led to one million deaths and the emigration of another two million people during the next ten years[1].

New sources of income were desperately needed. Irish women were well known for their needlework skills and at that time lace was in demand throughout the western world[2]. The Irish women began to produce, at a competitive price, crochet versions of the expensive needle laces and bobbin laces. Lace schools sprang up and Irish crochet developed as a new industry of economic importance during the famine and for many years afterwards, becoming the dominant Irish lace and employing many thousands of people.

The accounts of four people closely involved with Irish crochet in the nineteenth century provide a surprisingly detailed picture of the developments in the first 40 years.

John Frances Maguire (1815–72), Member of Parliament, Mayor of Cork and prolific author, wrote about the 1852 National Exhibition at Cork and the lace, crochet and needlework in nearby convents and special schools in his 1853 book, *The Industrial Movement in Ireland as Illustrated by the National Exhibition of 1852.*

Mrs Susanna Meredith (1823–1901), who found herself widowed at the age of 24 soon after the famine struck, began the Adelaide Lace School in Cork as a charitable venture. From this experience she wrote about the crocheters and Irish crochet in *The Lacemakers*, published in 1865.

The Dublin lace dealer Ben Lindsey (1829–93), prepared a catalogue for the Mansion House Exhibition of Irish lace in London in 1883 which included for the first time, photographs of the laces, making it a very valuable record. He reprinted the history and other photographs three years later[3].

A newspaper article attributed to Michael Holland (1855–1950) who worked for a crochet dealer in Cork in the 1880s gives some new information about the crochet industry[4].

Details of John Maguire and Mrs. Meredith are in Appendix I and of Ben Lindsey and Michael Holland later in the book.

I found further information in the reports of the various exhibitions at which lace was exhibited and in the books of the lace historians, Elizabeth Boyle (*The Irish Flowerers* of 1971), Mrs Bury Palliser (*A History of Lace* of 1865) and Santina Levey (*Lace: A History* of 1983).

Crocheting was known and practised in Ireland before the famine[5]. However, it was probably basic or ordinary crochet, used to make warm clothing rather than lace. Crochet was also being worked in France, Germany and Scandinavia as discussed in my other book[6].

The Nuns and other Benevolent Women in Cork and Southern Ireland

Ben Lindsey writes that the Irish crochet lace industry began at Cork at the time of the famine and was of great importance in saving the lives of many people[7].

Elizabeth Boyle[8] thought that crochet may have come to Cork in the 1790s with four Ursuline nuns, Irish girls returning to the newly established convent at Blackrock after completing their novitiate in Paris[9].

In 1845, the year the potato blight struck, the nuns at this convent began teaching Irish crochet lace to keep the children at their Poor School and provide them with an income. Otherwise their mothers kept them at home on the off-chance they could make money by doing messages for neighbours[10]. In that same year, a Mrs Dwyer of Cork paid £50 for crochet work and knitted purses made in the Poor School in 1845[11]. The payments to the children for their crochet grew from about £90 in 1846 to £1200 in 1852[12].

The children learnt quickly, were creative and had a flair for design. John Maguire gave the example of one girl of eight working an excellent collar, and another aged twelve or thirteen producing a 'most exquisite' design[13].

As the potato blight continued and the famine worsened, crochet became a valuable money-making skill and quickly spread throughout Co. Cork. It was soon taught in many convents and other special schools, many of which John Maguire described[14]. Among the 'benevolent ladies' who did so much to help the needy by running these schools were Miss Bergin, Miss Byrne, Miss Crofts, Lady Deane, Mrs Dwyer, Miss Foot, Mrs James Lyons, Mrs Manly, Miss Nano Nagle and Mrs Woodlocke[15]. Mrs Dwyer of Great Georges Street, Mrs Woodlocke, Mrs James Lyons, and Miss Byrne began the

Sisters of Mercy's School, St. Mary's Industrial School and the Orphan's School in Cork[16]. Mrs Manly, Miss Foot and the Misses Bergin and Crofts were also active in schools teaching crochet. By the end of the decade about 500–600 young crocheters around Blackrock were in constant work[17]

Only a few of the many other success stories told by John Maguire will be mentioned here. For example, 80 of the girls in the St. Mary's Industrial School begun by Mrs. Dwyer came out of the Workhouse and were able to support themselves 'in comfort and independence'[18].

Lady Deane's school was run strictly with a high standard of work and cleanliness. It obviously produced some superb work, as two sets of flounces, including one displayed in Sir Thomas Deane's case at the 1852 Exhibition in Cork, were sold for 25 guineas (£26.5.0)[19] .

Mrs Meredith's Adelaide Lace School in Cork also made a large contribution before it closed in 1859. There were 120 people involved at one time. It began as a day school and later expanded into a central depot, taking in lace which was sold directly to wholesalers in England[20].

Other schools which taught crochet in and around Cork included the South Presentation Poor School in Cork, started by Miss Honoria (Nano) Nagle, the Presentation Convent School at Youghal, the Cork Industrial School run by the established Church, and one run by the Sisters of Mercy at Kinsale[21].

John Maguire described some of the work produced in various schools and convents in the early 1850s as very beautiful imitations of exquisite and valuable pieces of old lace such as Point, Honiton, Venetian, Mechlin and Guipure, as well as other richly patterned fabrics handed down as family heirlooms[22].

Mrs. Roberts, the Teachers she Trained and the Wives of Clergymen Further North in Ireland

At this stage you may care to check the map at the front of the book. It includes all the counties but only a few of the main towns. The county is given with the names of the other towns mentioned in the text.

Further north, Mrs W.C. (Martha) Roberts [c.1801 –?] started teaching Irish crochet lace in about 1847 at Kilcullen in Co. Kildare. After six months of classes every day her most intelligent workers produced some admirable specimens from Guipure and Point de Venise laces. Everyone Mrs Roberts personally taught was required to teach three others, and so on, until hundreds had learnt to crochet. At one time there were 700 crocheters earning money from this lace in her area[23]. I found no information about where she learnt to crochet but it may have been in England where she was born[24].

Mrs Roberts wrote that she 'taught five poor women to copy the crochet spiders' in some poorly-designed lace with crabs and spiders that came to her from a friend in Dover. Mrs Roberts then lent the women 'different pieces of old lace – and of their own ingenuity they brought it to its present perfection'[25]. This suggests that she and her pupils may have developed with little or no outside help.

It appears that Mrs Roberts did not teach Irish crochet for long, as in 1848 her clergyman husband took up an appointment in England. We know from census records that from 1851 to 1861 the Roberts family lived at the vicarage in Edwardstone, Suffolk[26]. (Further information on the family appears in Appendix I.).

Twenty eight of Mrs Roberts' best workers went out as teachers[27]. One of the first, whose name is unknown, went to Mrs Cassandra Hand (?–1868), the wife of the rector in Clones, a market town in Co. Monaghan and began the long and distinguished history of Irish crochet lace in that area[28]. Many of the styles worked at Clones are shown in the following chapters[29].

Mrs Hand entered 'some specimens of work of "Crochet Guipure" produced for charitable purposes' in the 1853 Dublin Exhibition[30]. The Clones workers realized that she was a good businesswoman so when she wanted to retire in 1854, they persuaded her to stay for a few more years[31]. It appears that she learnt to crochet from Mrs Roberts' trainee, as the records say that she taught as well as managed the business. When Mrs Hand finally resigned, she handed over to a trained teacher who maintained high standards long after they had slipped in other areas. Even though this new teacher, an 'accomplished lady, ... had been trained in the best schools of art' and was obviously of considerable value to Clones crochet, we do not know her name either[32].

Another of Mrs Roberts' new teachers went to New Ross in Co. Wexford and did well under the supervision of Mrs Tottenham, the wife of the rector. Mrs Roberts praised Mrs Tottenham very highly and said that her pupils' work rivaled the antique laces they worked from. These two women were known in London for their very superior crochet[33].

Mrs. Maclean, the wife of the rector at Tynan in Co. Armagh probably learnt her Irish crochet through the Tottenhams, relations by marriage[34]. Mrs. McLean is better known these days for Inishmacsaint lace, an exquisite needle lace which she originated[35].

Mrs Martin, wife of the rector at Killeshandra, Co. Cavan, the next county to the west, started crochet Guipure in about 1847 and supervised its production there for 30 years. Miss Young then took over and in 1888 Old Point and Spanish Point dress trimmings, robings, table borders and furniture trimmings were advertised as available from a local cottage centre[36]. Two collars of early Irish crochet lace from Killeshandra are shown in the next chapter.

The Crochet Schools

Many of the crochet schools which were opened at the time of the famine were run by clergymen's wives and by convents. The few that survived made very important contributions, especially in the remote areas[37].

Mrs Meredith tells us that Irish crochet was usually done in groups with the skilled workers making the difficult motifs and the less skilled making the easier ones[38]. Still others tacked the motifs to the foundation and someone else crocheted the ground which joined the motifs. Children often did the simpler tasks. As might be expected with such crisis-job-creation-projects involving many people, there were often problems with poor work[39].

Although a number of young boys had attended Mrs Roberts' classes in Co. Kildare[40] at the time of the famine, it was usually the girls and young women who worked Irish crochet. For many of them it must have been a good way of earning a living. Some saved up to migrate, usually to America[41]. There were few alternatives[42].

The Early Designing

Attractive designs were obviously of crucial importance. In the early 1850s the principal of the Ursuline Convent at Blackrock, Co. Cork did most of the designing for a collection going to a New York Exhibition[43]. It seems that Lady Deane may have helped with the designing in her school[44]. In the Adelaide Lace School at Cork the pupils did some of the designing[45] and at the very least they made the adaptations needed to translate the antique laces into crochet. Both Mrs Meredith and John Maguire wrote of their talent. Mrs Roberts gave credit to her early pupils for their contributions, as mentioned earlier, p. 12.

Crochet is a particularly versatile craft and the girls used this freedom to produce some original, extraordinary and very complicated shapes[46]. As might be expected, regional differences developed in the lace; the Cork and Clones crocheters maintained their own distinctive features[47].

On a different level, a delightful collection of professional designs for Irish crochet lace and other needlework was published in 1853 by the English thread company, Marslands, in *Marslands Manual of New and Improved Registered Designs in Crochet, Guipure, Lacet and Embroidery Work.* Two of the designs appear on p. 13 of the companion volume, *Mademoiselle Riego and Irish Crochet*[48]. We know that this company traded in Ireland as their thread was displayed in the 1853 Exhibition in Dublin[49] and they ordered a shamrock edging from one of the Irish crochet schools[50].

I have not seen any Irish crochet made in the style of Marslands designs which is not surprising. Their manual gave only drawings and most crocheters needed to see worked pieces such as were often sewn onto fabric pages of a sample book[51]. One example of such a book is shown by Ada Longfield[52] and another is in the Ulster Folk and Transport Museum, Holywood, Co. Down, Northern Ireland.

The 1853 Dublin Exhibition

The 1853 Dublin Exhibition probably displayed some of the best early work. The listing in Appendix II provides a useful record of the type of articles worked in crochet lace at the time. Highlights included entry 863, an infant's cap and robe in finest crochet 'point' and caps, collars and sleeves &c. in crochet guipure from Mrs Ryan, Inch House, Borrisoleigh, Co. Tipperary and entry 868, 'a double point crochet berthe, lappets, sleeves &c.' from the children of the Industrial School of the Sisters of Mercy, Lower Baggot St, Dublin. This list also shows the areas in which crochet lace was being worked in Ireland and elsewhere[52].

Marketing and Economic Value

Irish crochet lace was fashionable in Britain while the public felt sorry for the Irish. Even royalty wore the better pieces[54].

It was certainly of great economic value, as around Clones 'the crochet harvest was only second in importance to the grain crop'. Mrs Meredith quoted figures of about £144,000 for lace exports and £1,400,000 for sewed muslin in the early 1860s. She wrote of 20,000 workers in the indigenous laces which were by then dominated by crochet[55].

Substantial amounts of crochet were sold first in London and later in Europe, America, India and Australia[56]. There were considerable quantities of crochet at the Great Exhibition of 1851 in London[57].

The Decline in the Post Famine Period

Irish crochet began to decline after about 1857 because of bad work, poor management, unscrupulous tradesmen and problems in managing the girls who could be very difficult[58].

There are only a few reports of Irish crochet lace in the late 1860s and 1870s. By 1869 sales of crochet and lace at Kenmare in Co. Kerry had reached the sum of £500[59]. Mrs Bury Palliser, a London lace expert, was disappointed in the Irish crochet at the London International Exhibition of 1874, writing that the very fine, superior crochet from Ireland had been replaced by cheap, coarse material. The workers were not interested in doing the higher quality pieces[60].

Two of the few surviving lace and crochet schools of this time are worth mentioning. Miss Pedder's School for the Employment of Industrious Poor Cottage Women in Co. Tipperary, is on record as producing crochet caps in beautiful old Point Guipure, and other lace work in 1874[61].

Up north at Lissadell in Co. Sligo, Lady Gore-Booth started a crochet school in about 1879. Tenants and workers on the Gore-Booth estate were taught crochet, white embroidery and drawn-thread work. They produced collars, christening dresses, table linens and other household goods in the 1880s and 1890s. Her son, Sir Josslyn Gore-Booth, later ran this enterprise as a cooperative[62].

Cork Crochet

Both Mrs. Meredith and Ben Lindsey had a low opinion of the crochet from Cork, saying that with a few exceptions it was plain and simple[63].

On the other hand, an 1889 newspaper report attributed to Michael Holland gave a good account of Cork crochet in the 1860s and 1880s. It claimed that even though the south of Ireland had long been recognized as the principal seat of Irish crochet, the industry had not been run in a business-like way[64]. Keep in mind that Mrs Meredith closed her Adelaide Lace School in 1859, apparently for lack of interest.

The article tells us that in about 1860, the two dealers in Cork exported large quantities of crochet to England. The standard was excellent and prices were good until machine-made laces came in from Europe. In 1889 the main exports were antimacassars, bedspreads, d'oyleys and cushion covers in coarse threads along with collars and laces in fine threads. Collars and d'oyleys were always in demand.

The official report on the Cork Exhibition of 1883 was along similar lines. Dwyer & Co., Michael Holland's employer exhibited 'a very good case, worthy of notice for careful work and design and worthy of a medal'. The other dealer, T. Lyons & Co., entered 'a general crochet case, very good work, very effective for general sale, being selected from a large stock and not made specially for exhibition; second in merit'[65]. Dwyer & Co. was also well known in America in the 1880s for high quality goods[66].

These dealers bought crochet from the districts around Cork and in the nearby counties of Limerick and Waterford. Export figures for 1880 amounted to £18,000 but declined to about £9,000 by 1886[66].

CHAPTER 2
Early Laces to 1858

As I delved further into the history, I was delighted to find that even after more than 150 years, several of the styles of Irish crochet worked shortly after the famine could be identified with some confidence. There are known dates of acquisition of a few laces by the Victoria & Albert Museum and an Irish convent. The combination of information from early books, exhibitions, portraits and trends from costume history placed some styles in this general time period[1].

Spanish Point Imitations

This style, made at Clones, was based on laces which came onto the market after the Spanish monasteries were dissolved in 1830[2]. The bold motifs have padded rings in the centre, large arches and in some cases simple needle lace fillings.

The border in Fig 2.1 which was shown in the 1883 Mansion House Exhibition has two types of shamrocks and an incomplete circle with peaks round the edge, a tail and picots on the radial bars[2] in a background of simple intersecting picot loops. The lower edge is of heavier loops with picots.

Library of Trinity College Dublin

Fig 2.1. Part of a border in the Spanish Point style, 1883[2].

Two portraits from the 1850s show this style of lace.

The mother's collar in the painting, Fig 2.2 has a motif similar to the incomplete circle with peaks in Figure 2.1[3].

V&A Images, Victoria & Albert Museum

Fig 2.2. Good Morning, Mama painted by S.B. Halle in 1859[4] features Spanish Point Imitation motifs in the mother's collar.

The cylindrical lace cuffs with large bold motifs set in a fine ground in the portrait of an Italian woman, Fig 2.3, have been identified as crochet lace by Santina Levey[5]. There is a shamrock on the left hand cuff, close to the dog.

Uffizi Gallery, Florence

Fig 2.3. This 1850s portrait of an Italian woman, Luisa Grace Barolino, by an unknown artist includes cuffs in the Spanish Point Imitation style.

Some of the accessories fashionable in the 1850s and 1860s were in this bold motif style of Irish crochet – for example, berthas, cylindrical cuffs, headwear such as fall caps and fanchons, also large sleeves. A bertha or berthe is an off-the-shoulder collar; a fall cap has a more or less circular piece on top of the head with lappets or streamers coming down over the ears, whereas a fanchon is triangular. Serious lace historians may care to check the dates in the notes at the back of the book and look up some of these examples[6].

Mme German Hardouin, who wrote six large Irish crochet pattern books in French in the early 1900s, identified many motifs used in the early Irish crochet. Three of them which have some similarity to motifs in Fig 2.1 are shown below in Fig 2.4a, b and c. Note the curved stem of the shamrock in c.

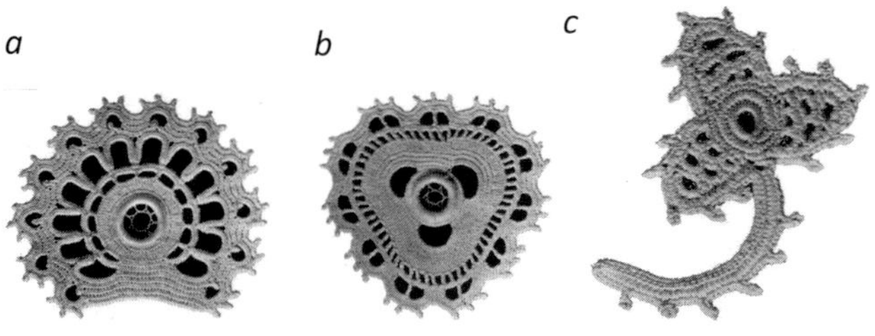

Library of the Author

Fig 2.4 Three of Mme Hardouin's old motifs
a 'Deuxième séries étoiles No 2'
b 'Deuxième séries étoiles No 4, a shamrock.
c. Série de petits motifs, another shamrock

Guipure

The Guipure styles were taught in schools supervised by the wives of various clergymen from about 1847, firstly by Mrs Roberts in Co. Kildare, then by Mrs Hand at Clones, Co. Monaghan[8] and by Mrs Martin, nearby at Killeshandra, Co. Cavan[9]. They were usually worked in very fine thread[10].

The term Guipure usually means a lace without a mesh ground[11] but the Irish crochet version is quite different, presumably because of some confusion with the names of the traditional laces used as design sources in the early days.

Ben Lindsey described three forms of Guipure which all have either horseshoe-, crescent- or Y-shaped structures surrounded by shells and picot loops[12].

Knotted Guipure, (Fig 2.5), involved 'knotting the threads as the work of knitting them together proceed[ed]' and required considerable skill[12].

It has large horseshoes, filled with shells of mesh and tiny padded rings in an irregular ground mostly of stars with six spokes and picots, quite different to the grounds in the English and European pattern books[13].

I have unable to find knots in any of the pieces I have seen and suspect that the style was simplified over time. The summary at the end of this chapter has a little more comment on this lace.

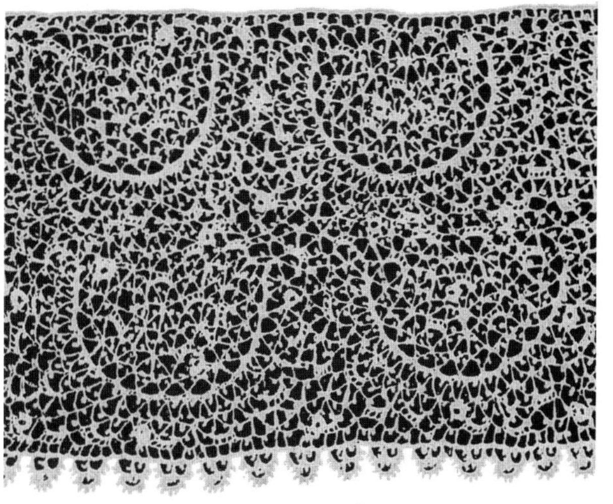

British Library Board All Rights Reserved MIC 9248 (b)

Fig 2.5 A section of a Knotted Guipure border which was included in Ben Lindsey's 1886 book.

Mme Hardouin and Mary Card both gave instructions for working this complicated style which they called horseshoe lace. The horseshoe was often worked over one or two strands of relatively fine cord to assist in the shaping and formed a motif which could be tacked onto a foundation pattern for joining. It requires a good deal of skill and is so irregular that Mary Card wrote of it as uncopyable[14].

Knotted Guipure, the most commonly seen of this group, was used for fichus, collars, fanchons and handkerchiefs, some of which were in vogue in the 1850s and are shown in other books[15].

Lifted Guipure (Fig 2.6), had its stitches 'lifted in the working' and this was said to be more difficult than knotting. Its value was in its 'solidity while a light and elegant appearance was maintained'. It was also said to be 'exceedingly durable but was not always appreciated'[16]. I have not found any directions for working this style.

The early illustrations and the few examples I have seen show only the common crochet techniques.

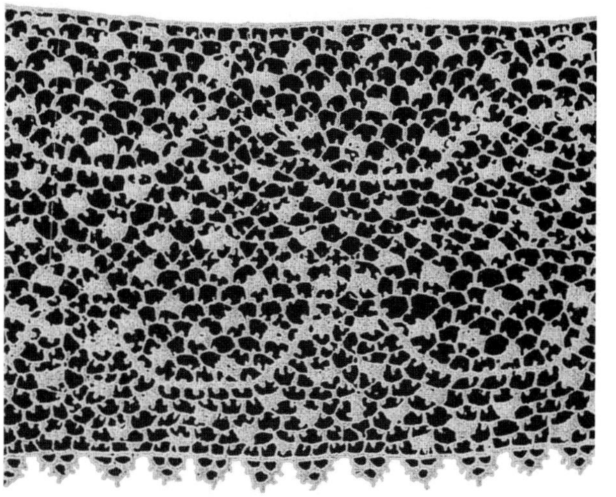

British Library Board All Rights Reserved MIC 9248 (b)

Fig 2.6 Lifted Guipure from Ben Lindsey's 1886 book.

Imitation Guipure (Fig 2.7), has triplets or Y-shaped stems with a range of end pieces (sometimes shamrocks).

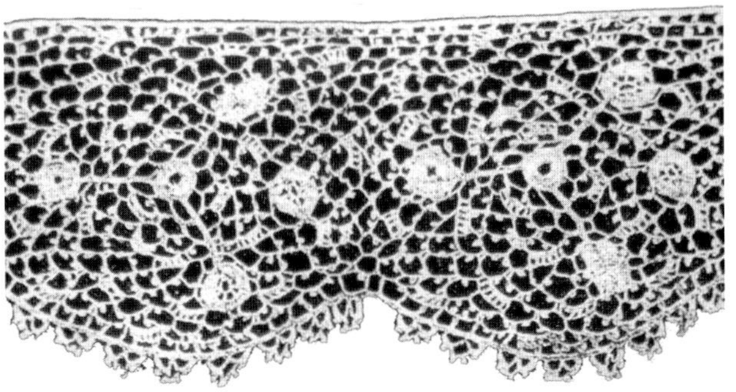

Library of Trinity College Dublin

Fig 2.7 Part of an Imitation Guipure border as shown in the London Mansion House Exhibition of 1883[17].

Mme Hardouin and Mary Card both gave instructions for working it, and I have seen a few examples in private collections[18]. As with the Knotted Guipure it is worked in motifs which are tacked onto a foundation for joining.

Lace with Meandering Lines Joining Motifs often in a Complex Irregular Ground

Shamrocks, Rings and other Simple Motifs

Two pieces in this style can be dated back to 1853 when they came into the Victoria & Albert Museum, London.

The collar in Fig 2.8 has twisting lines with end pieces like the shamrocks and rings of the Imitation Guipure just described. Four-leafed shamrocks are also present. The ground is simple and irregular with few picots. The other example in the Museum is a cylindrical sleeve ruffle, 1853.V875, but it is so similar to the collar that it not included in this book.

V&A Images, Victoria & Albert Museum

Fig 2.8 Simple collar with shamrock motifs 1853 .V876 (48[circumference] x 6.5cm)

The records of the Museum do not indicate where this collar was worked or bought.

I have seen a few examples of this style in the literature, on the internet and in museums. Attractive and more intricate collars and a flounce in this style are in the National Museum of Ireland and in the Ulster Folk and Transport Museum[19].

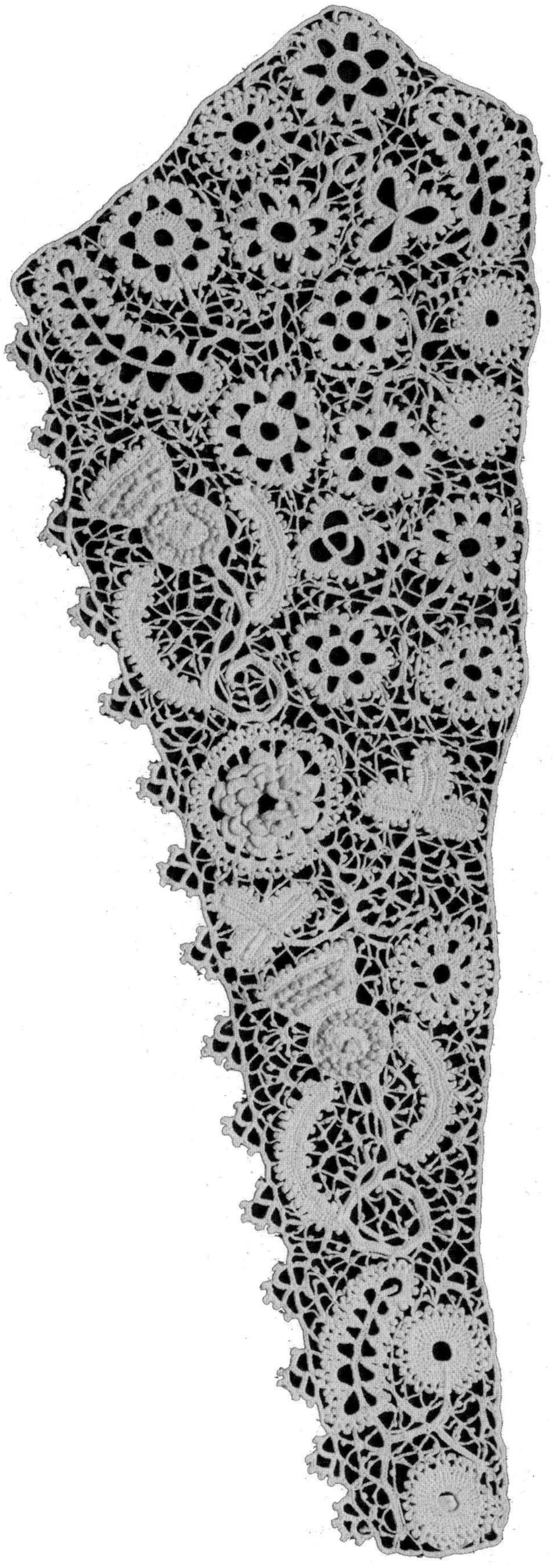

V&A Images, Victoria & Albert Museum

Fig 2.9 A lapel 1854.V1095 (38.5 x 13 cm

Rose, Thistle, Shamrock and Other Intricate Motifs

The lapel in Fig 2.9, on the left, which was acquired by the Victoria & Albert Museum in 1854 has the same meandering stems but is much more complex[20]. It features a raised rose, thistles and shamrocks, along with other motifs in a complicated ground with six-spoked stars similar to those in the Knotted Guipure, Fig 2.5.

Large, Heavy Irregular Floral and Grotesque Motifs in a Sparse Ground

The collars shown in Figs 2.10 and 2.11 on the next page are from Killeshandra, Co. Cavan, where Mrs Martin taught for many years after the famine, p. 12. They were acquired by the Victoria & Albert Museum in 1855.

They differ from each other only in the details of the motifs, which are generally floral, shamrock or grotesque with radiating fingers. Otherwise the grounds, edges and overall shapes of the collars are much the same.

The large, elaborate and irregular motifs in these collars are common in Irish crochet. The edges of some of them have often been worked over cord and are in high relief. Some of the motifs are solid, a few are of a fine mesh and others have solid and mesh areas alternating. This feature of some of the needle laces was reproduced in the crochet versions. Padded rings have been used as fillers in the second collar, Fig 2.12.

In 1859 Mrs Pullan described Irish crochet as a 'most tedious and complicated sort of work, consisting of heavy flowers, arabesques and other designs connected by ... bars'[21]. In her book of old Irish lace motifs Mme Hardouin included a series of motifs which she called 'arabesque', with radiating fingers side by side. Two of them resemble some of the motifs in these Killeshandra collars [22].

The unusual open ground has only a few bars which usually go directly from one motif to another without intersecting and they include, for the first time in this series, Clones knots.

V&A Images, Victoria & Albert Museum

Fig 2.10 Gently scalloped collar with large motifs. 1855.V1159 (71 [circumference] x 10 cm)

V&A Images, Victoria & Albert Museum

Fig 2.11 Gently scalloped collar with different motifs to Fig 2.10. 1855.V1158 (51 [circumference] x 9 cm).

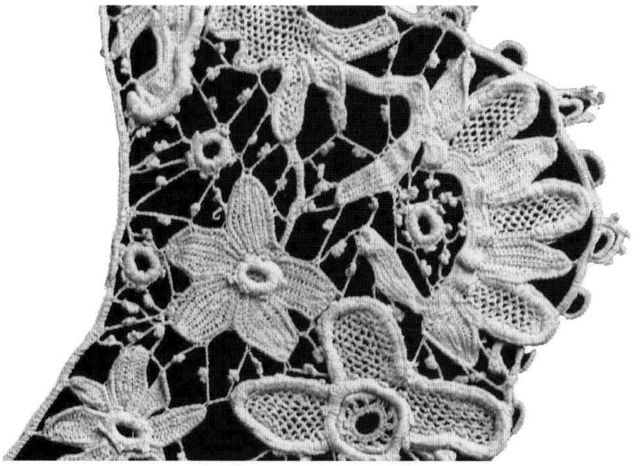

V&A Images, Victoria & Albert Museum

Fig 2.12 Detail of Fig 2.11. Note the Clones knots on the bars of the ground joining the motifs.

Mixed Style

The large and ambitious altar fall below, was worked by the children of Gardiner Street, Dublin and presented to the Mother Superior of the Sisters of Charity, Mary Aikenhead, at Dublin in May 1858[23]. The part on display behind glass at the Mary Aikenhead Heritage Centre measures about 60 x 45 cm, although the complete lace is probably about 7m long.

The cross is surrounded by leaves (including shamrocks), flat flowers, then bunches of flat grapes with tendrils and matching leaves. The lower border features the type of bold arched motifs seen in Figs 2.1–5 often with padded ring centres.

The simple shamrocks and the flat flowers on the outside of the oval around the centre are similar to motifs seen in other Irish crochet, but the open mesh leaves are unusual. Among the large bold arched motifs in the lower border is one (just right of centre) with peaks around an incomplete circle, as seen earlier in Figs 2.1, 2.2 and 2.4a in the Spanish Point group. Small irregular crescents appear above these border motifs.

Photograph taken by the Author

Fig 2.13. Part of an altar fall worked for the Novitiate Chapel of the Religious Sisters of Charity in Dublin.

The detail of the ground of chain loops, with what appear to be Clones knots is shown in Fig 2.15.

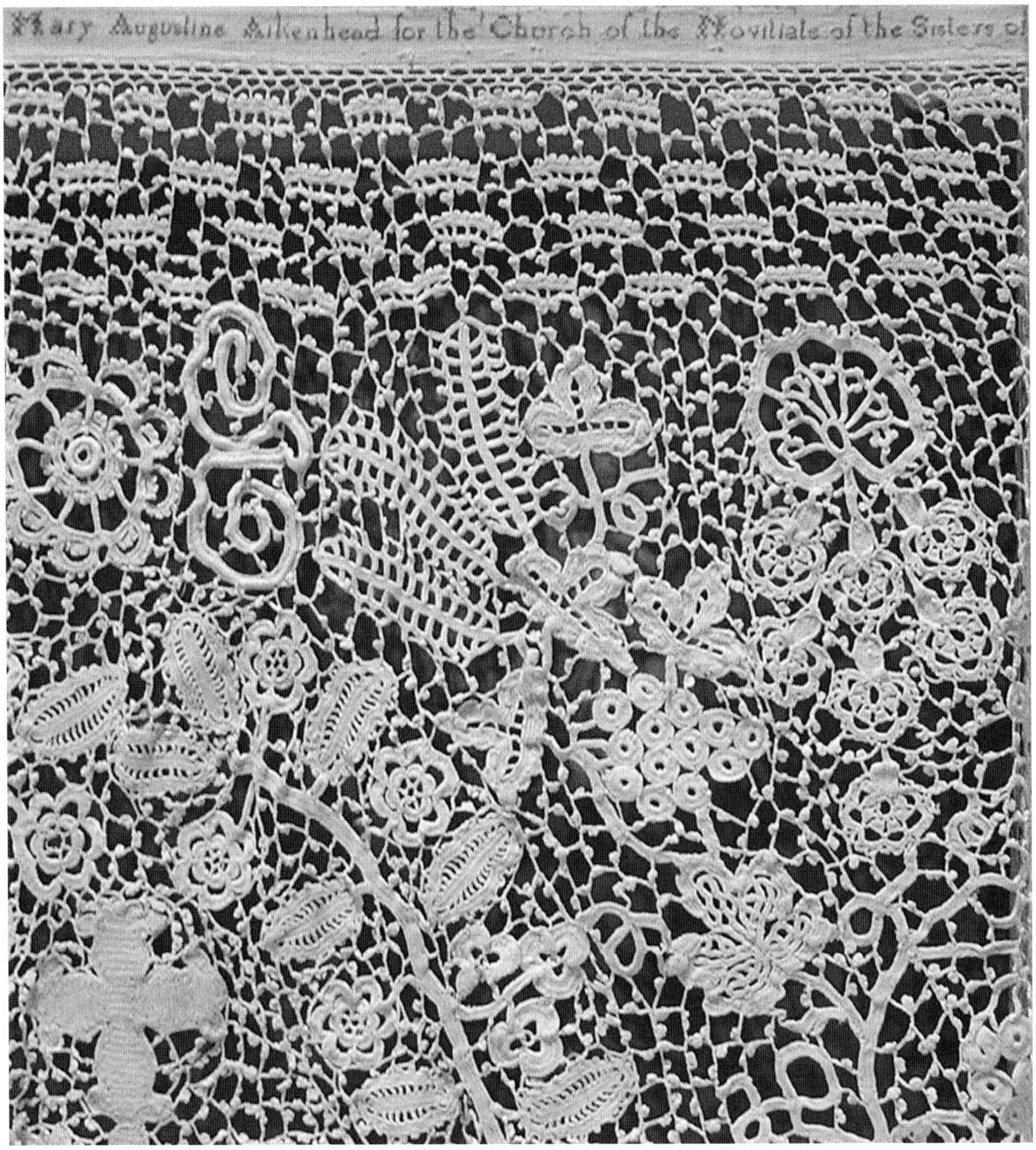

Photograph taken by the Author

Fig. 2.14 This close up shows the top right hand side of the altar fall in Fig 2.13.

The laces in this chapter share some features, especially shamrocks which were in the Spanish Point lace (Fig 2.1), in the collar (Fig. 2.10) and in the altar fall (Fig 2.14). They were also present as end pieces on the stems in the Imitation Guipure (Fig 2.7) and in the shamrock collar which came into the Victoria & Albert Museum in 1853, (Fig 2.8).

Large bold motifs, commonly with a padded ring centre were featured in both the Spanish Point Imitations in Fig 2.12.4 and along the lower border of the altar fall in Fig 2.13.

The time-consuming ground with six-spoked stars was present both in the Knotted Guipure (Figs 2.5 and 2.6) and the lapel with the rose, thistle and shamrocks (Fig 2.10).

Clones knots were used in Figs 2.10 - 14.

A raised rose was in the lapel, Fig 2.9, although it was a little different to the usual one.

Most of the laces were made in the traditional way of tacking motifs worked separately onto a foundation pattern and then filling in the ground.

Many of the motifs were worked over cord.

We know that the Spanish Point Imitations and Guipure styles were crocheted around Clones, the two collars with large floral and grotesque motifs were from nearby Killeshandra and the altar fall was made in Dublin.

The books of Eithne d'Arcy and Máire Treanor, Irish crocheters of Clones[24] included examples of the Spanish Point style but none of the Guipure laces. This is not surprising as they were technically demanding, were worked in very fine thread and the Knotted Guipure, the most popular of the group, is irregular and very hard if not impossible to copy.

CHAPTER 3
Other Styles of Possible Early Origin from The National Museum of Ireland and The Books of Ben Lindsey

This chapter considers five laces in the collection of the National Museum of Ireland and six from the books of Ben Lindsey. Some of them came into the Museum in 1880, a few were in the catalogue which Ben Lindsey and Harry Biddle prepared for the Mansion House Exhibition in London in 1883 and others were included in Ben Lindsey's book published three years later[1]. Two laces of uncertain age have been added, mainly because they are superb examples of Irish crochet lace. Some of the laces in the National Museum of Ireland which are particularly elaborate are shown in great detail.

Irish Lacet

Two flounces supplied by Ben Lindsey, Figs 3.1 and 3.2, show a new feature, oval motifs with an outer raised frame and crochet or needle lace fillings in the centre. I believe that this is the Irish Lacet style which Mrs. Bury Palliser wrote about in 1865[2]. She described it as of 'great beauty' and worked in linen thread with 'flowers and patterns filled in with lace stitches of admirable finish [in a] ground work of crochet'. Lacet in that era meant tape lace joined with a range of filling stitches made by a sewing needle[3] and the fillings in the flounce shown below are the most intricate, varied and unusual I have ever seen. As this was the only type of Irish crochet she mentioned, it may have been common in the mid 1860s.

The first example, Fig 3.1, has oval motifs with peaks on the outside and various crochet fillings inside. Other motifs include large heavily padded grotesque forms with complex and unusual needle lace fillings as well as flowers and leaves. The ground between them includes Clones knots which add to the richness.

This image is reproduced with the kind permission of the National Museum of Ireland

Fig 3.1 This flounce from Clones was supplied by Ben Lindsey in 1880. 1880.795 (12.5 cm deep).

The other flounce in the Irish lacet style, Fig 3.2, has grotesque motifs with small padded rings on the surface and several different crochet fillings. The ground joining them has a new feature, tiny semi-circles with picots on the bars. Again it came into the National Museum of Ireland in 1880.

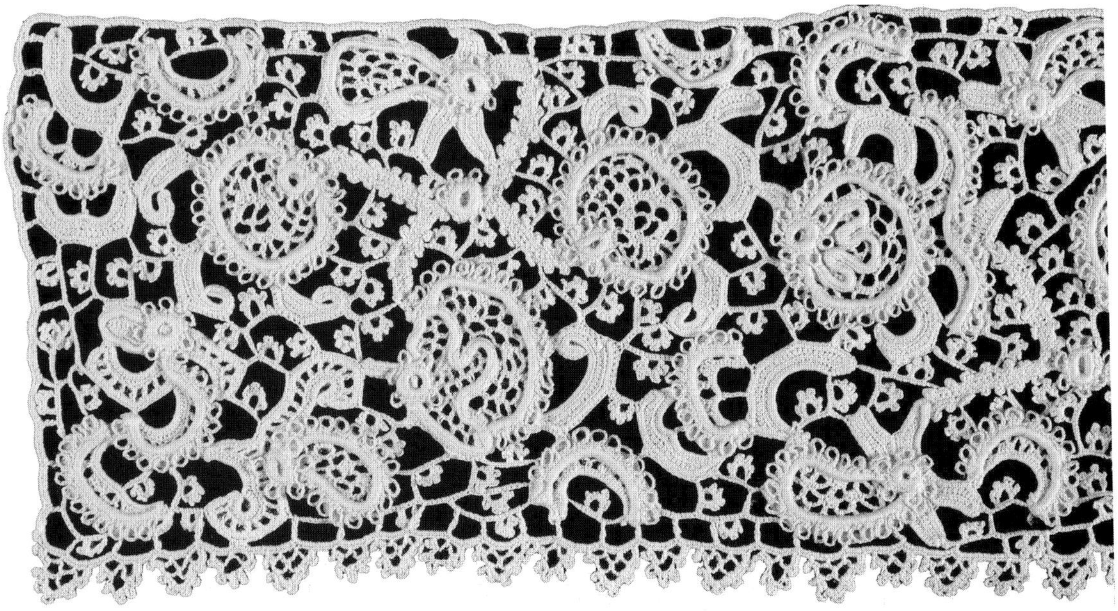

This image is reproduced with the kind permission of the National Museum of Ireland

Fig 3.2 Another flounce from Clones supplied by Ben Lindsey. 1880.794 (10.5 cm deep).

Greek Lace or Reticella

A third flounce, this time from Ben Lindsey's book, is in the style known as Greek lace, Fig 3.3, because it was copied almost perfectly from the Greek or Reticella needle laces which featured geometric designs with square divisions[4].

From the O'Kelley Collection, Special Collections, UCD Library, Dublin

Fig 3.3 A deep flounce of Greek or reticella lace from the 1883 Mansion House Exhibition.

This style was used as a trim on linen and furniture rather than on clothing[4].

Venetian Point

Ben Lindsey noted that the Point de Venise style of Irish crochet was among the earliest worked by Mrs Roberts in Co. Kildare and was also made at Clones[5]. It was so successfully copied that some of the crochet versions could scarcely be distinguished from the best examples of the original needle lace and of course had been worked at much less cost. The leaders of fashion in Paris, New York, Vienna and Brussels used it freely[6].

There are many types of Venetian lace such as Gros Point, Rose Point and Flat Point[7]. The names Venetian Point, Venetian lace, and Point de Venise, even Italian Point, given to the Irish crochet were probably used very loosely.

The Jesuit religious order provided the Clones crocheters with some particularly rich Venetian laces which were the inspiration for a style which became known as Jesuit lace. The early crochet in this style was 'very effective and greatly admired' but was difficult to work as you can see from Fig 3.4[8]. It has extensive raised surface work and many padded rings. Some motifs appear to have a simple needlelace filling in the centre. The ground has groups of picots along the bars.

Library of Trinity College Dublin

Fig 3.4 A Jesuit lace in the 1883 Mansion House Exhibition.

The Crochet Imitation Venetian Point in Fig 3.5, is unusual with open motifs of curves, circles and ovals in an almost geometric picot ground.

From the O'Kelley Collection, Special Collections, UCD Library, Dublin

Fig 3.5 Crochet Imitation Venetian Point in Ben Lindsey's 1886 book.

Crochet with L[illegible]e Stitch

The Crochet with Lace St[illegible] in Fig 3.6 is the first example we know is t[illegible] [I]t is in a very different style and the ground w[illegible] [wi]th a needle rather than with a crochet hook[9]. [illegible] [sha]mrocks, thistles, rings, non descript round mo[illegible] [me]dels, solid ovals and flowers with narrow petals as well as the raised rose. Some of the motifs are in triplets and others are on long stems, which are sometimes looped. There are small simple wheels scattered through the border and along the lower side.

British Library Board All Rights Reserved MIC A 9248 (b)

Fig 3.6 A flounce in Crochet with Lace Stitch shown in Ben Lindsey's 1886 book.

The collar in this style shown in Fig 3.7 has many of the same motifs as Fig. 3.6, including the raised rose.

This image is reproduced with the kind permission of the National Museu[illegible]

Fig 3.7. A collar in the style called Crochet with Lace Stitch from Bantry in Co. Cork 1972-8 T123.

This Crochet with Lace Stitch is much simpler than the Irish crochet seen so far. It has easy little motifs which would have been suitable for the beginners and young children who were put to work in the famine years[10]. Women who had done sewn muslin work before the famine may have found the needle lace ground easier to work than the crocheted version, which could be difficult[11].

At the beginning of the book, p. 6, I referred to the much-quoted claim that the English needlework designer, Mlle Riego, 'invented' Irish crochet. Yet a[ll] the facts presented so far indicate that the Irish workers used the traditional needle and bobbin laces as sources of design. Now, in the Crochet with Lace Stitch we encounter for the first time, three motifs which are similar to some in the English pattern books of the late 1840s and early 1850s, are shown in detail in Fig 3.8.

The thistles in a triplet marked 'a' on the left side of Fig 3.6 are very like those in Fig 3.8a from Mlle Riego's 1849 Crochet Collar - British emblems[12].

Corrections for Early History of Irish Crochet Lace, Page 22 paragraph 2, Fig 2.12.4 should be Fig 2.1-4 and paragraph 3 the last Figure is 2.9 not 2.10.

Similarly, one of the shamrocks, marked 'b' on the left side of Fig 3.6, resembles the one in Fig 3.8b from *Carter's Royal Exhibition Knitting, Netting and Crochet Book,* probably published in about 1850. The distinctive features are the thin triangular centre and simple leaflets.

The leaf with the open point in the group of three marked 'c' on the lower border of Fig 3.6, is similar to leaf Fig 3.8c from the same book. It is not as distinctive as the thistle and shamrock and may have been created independently of W. Carter's book. However, the fact that these three motifs occur together in the same style of lace suggests that the pattern books were the source, especially as their illustrations were quite large.

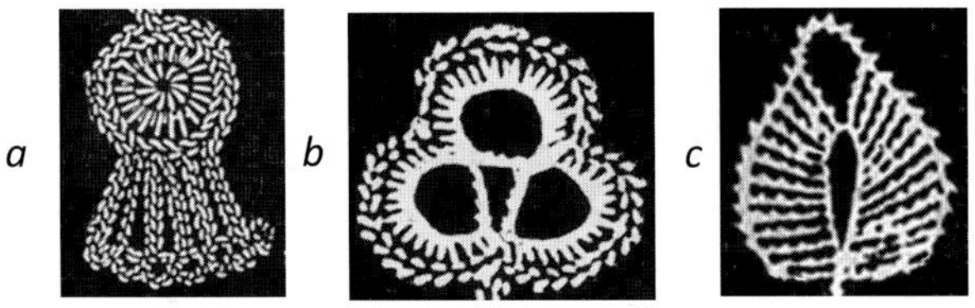

Fig 3.8 Motifs from pattern books of the late 1840s and early 1850s. Thistle **a** *is a Mlle Riego design of 1849 and leaves* **b** *and* **c** *are from W. Carter's book of about 1851.*

The only firm date for this style is 1886 when Ben Lindsey's book was published, but other information raises the possibility of an earlier origin. Three of the motifs resemble some in pattern books of the late 1840s and early 1850s. Roses, thistles and shamrocks were often used together in needlework designs of the early 1850s. Some of the many collars in this style which have survived are of types worn in the 1850s or 1860s[13].

Mixed Styles

Figure 3.9 shows another example from Cork, almost primitive and rather mixed with large, bold, corded motifs similar to the Spanish Point style seen on p. 15. There are two types of shamrocks, one of which has an elaborate filling. The very large thistle has a padded ring centre, the round motifs have large arches, the almost solid circles have a picot edge and the fan has seven solid radiating spikes joined for most of their length. The motifs have looped stems like some of those in Fig 3.6.

Library of Trinity College, Dublin

Fig 3.9 Lace Crochet from Cork in the Mansion House Exhibition.

The fan motif at the centre along the top of this lace resembles Fig 3.10 from Mme Hardouin's book of old Irish crochet lace motifs[14]. It is often seen in Irish crochet.

Library of the Author

Fig 3.10 Fan from Série de Combinaisons, No 1 as given by Mme Hardouin.

Another example from Cork as shown in the Mansion House Exhibition is presented below. It is very different to the usual Irish crochet being worked to a set pattern with medallions joined in the working. It does not appear to involve the use of cord.

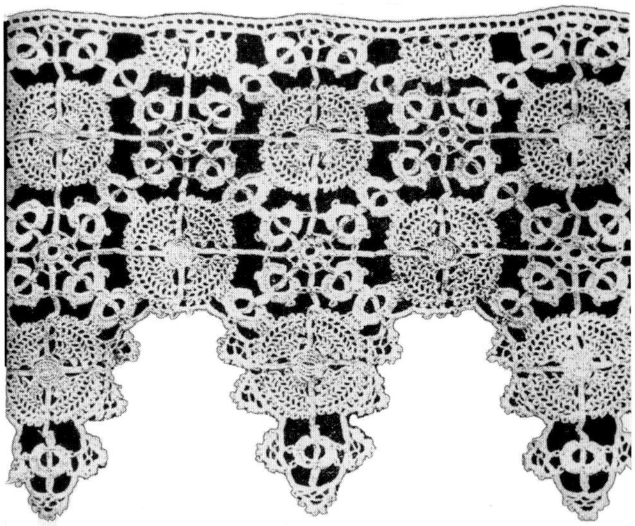

Library of Trinity College Dublin

Fig 3.11 Plain Crochet, Cork in the 1883 Mansion House Exhibition.

The laces from Clones seen up to this point, Figs 2.1, 2.5, 2.6, 2.7, and one of the Cork group, Fig 3.9 resemble the traditional needle laces but the other Cork laces are different. They are plain and simple, just as Mrs Meredith and John Maguire described the Irish crochet from Cork in the previous chapter, p 14.

The Crochet with Lace Stitch, Figs 3.6 and 3.7 worked without cord and with a needle lace ground is relatively common, particularly in small neat collars, and I have also seen it used in a handkerchief. I have not encountered any lace resembling the other two Cork laces Figs 3.9 and 3.11. However, the example based on medallions would not normally be recognized as Irish crochet.

Beautiful Examples of Irish Crochet

John Maguire, Mrs. Meredith and Ben Lindsey[15] described some of the early Irish crochet as beautiful. Because none of the illustrations looked at so far reflected this to my satisfaction, I have included two more examples from the National Museum of Ireland in Figs 3.12 and 3.13. They have features which are consistent with an early origin..

The flounce shown in Fig 3.12 appears to be in the Irish lacet style which was worked in the 1860s.

It is a superbly worked, very fine lace described in the Museum records as Imitation Italian Raised Point. Some of the shamrock and grotesque motifs with raised work over cord have simple crochet fillings. Others have cobweb needle lace fillings reminiscent of the Irish Lacet style, p. 23. Small flowers are used as fillers. The lower, scalloped side has one of the traditional looped edges and the straight upper side has unusual exceedingly fine, large, open picots.

This image is reproduced with the kind permission of the National Museum of Ireland

Fig 3.12 A deep flounce of Imitation Italian Raised Point. 1915.252 (17 cm deep)

The final lace in this chapter has heavily padded motifs which include shamrocks, some with a simple crochet filling and fans with radiating spikes, as well as the 'arabesques' or fingers side by side which are similar to those which Mme Hardouin believed were of early origin, Figs 2.12 and 13. Collars with deep angular points were fashionable in the mid 1850s and I expect the matching cuffs of that period also had such peaks. This cuff was worked in very fine thread.

This image is reproduced with the kind permission of the National Museum of Ireland

Fig 3.13 Half of one of a pair of elaborate cuffs. 1936. 26 T152 (7.5 cm deep).

The new features of the laces in this chapter include:

Motifs consisting of a frame with complex needle lace or crochet fillings which I believe are the Irish Lacet which Mrs. Bury Palliser wrote about in 1865.

Geometric designs based on a square (Greek or reticella).

Fans made of up to eight spikes joined for most of their length and elaborate grounds such as the one in Figs 3.2 with semi circles on the bars and Fig 3.4 which has groups of picots.

Large picots grouped in clusters in the ground as in Fig 3.4.

We see laces from Cork for the first time. One was geometric and composed of medallions without any ground but the other two were almost primitive with a range of motifs, which included flowers, thistles and shamrocks, which were sometimes in groups of three and with looped or curved stems.

Three of the motifs in the Crochet with Lace Stitch, Fig 3.8 resembled some in the pattern books of Mlle Riego and W. Carter, published in the late 1840s and early 1850s. This simple lace would have been a suitable one for children and beginners to make.

Features of the laces in Chapter 2 were also seen, such as the heavy bold motifs with large arches, radiating fingers (arabesques) and shamrocks. Strangely-shaped and complicated grotesque motifs of the general type seen in the Killeshandra collars, Figs 2.10 to 2.12, p 20. and in the Introduction to Irish Crochet techniques, p. 9 were present in Fig 3.1. However, none of grounds included the many-spoked stars, of Figs 2.5 and 2.9 nor the shells seen in the Guipure styles, Figs 2.5, 2.6 and 2.7.

Chapter 4
Irish Crochet Lace Similar to Madame Goubaud's Point Lace Imitations of the Late 1860s and The History of the Raised Rose

Madame Goubaud's Point Lace Imitations

As you will recall from Chapter 1, Irish crochet had declined by the 1860s. The little that was being made in Ireland was often poorly designed and worked. However there is a style which resembles the d'oyleys in *Madame Goubaud's Crochet Book* published in 1869 which we need to consider.

I suspect that Mme Marie Goubaud edited rather than wrote the comprehensive series of needlework books published under her name. These books were reprinted in *Beeton's Book of Needlework* in 1870 giving them a much wider circulation. As Mme Goubaud was French and lived in Paris, her 'Point Lace Imitation' d'oyleys may have been a French variant of Irish crochet. They were, after all, not called Irish crochet. Two of the d'oyleys are shown in my other book, *Mademoiselle Riego and Irish Crochet Lace*[1].

The motifs for Mme Goubaud's d'oyleys were worked without cord and were put together without any ground. The example shown in Fig 4.1 is similar to hers in that it features raised roses, groups of leaflets on crossed stems and other nondescript round motifs, many of which have been used in other Irish crochet. In addition, the overall effect is not appealing because of the poor design and the distorted motifs.

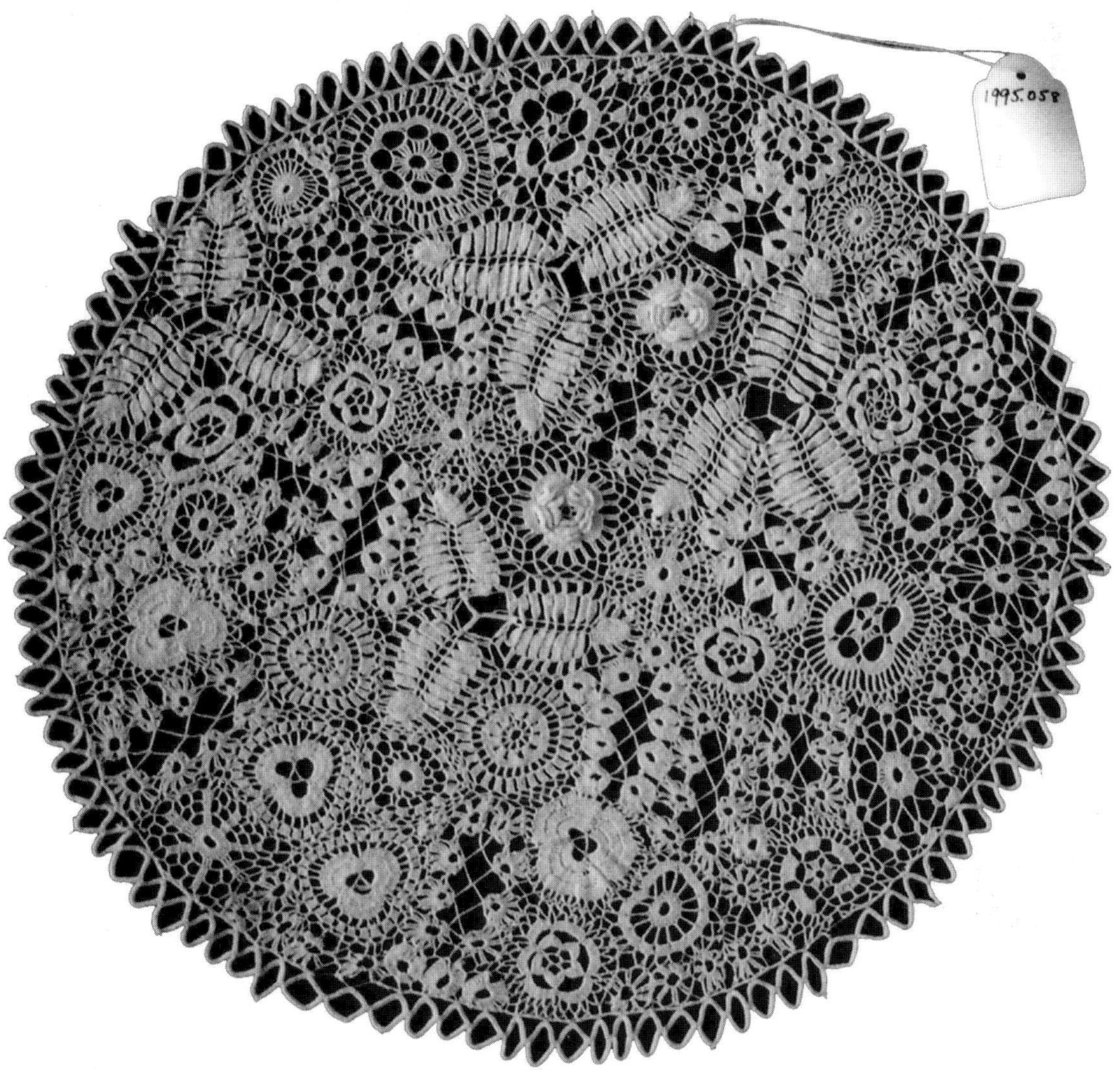

Embroiderers' Guild of Western Australia

Fig 4.1 Large d'oyley or Centrepiece. 1995.05.08 (22 x 22 cm)

This d'oyley also includes two motifs which resemble some in the English pattern books. The shamrocks in the upper left have the thin triangular centre seen before in the Crochet with Lace Stitch, Fig 3.9, and in W. Carter's pattern book of the early 1850s (p.26). The large group of three 'leaves' around the centre also resemble motifs in Mlle Riego's patterns from the 1840s[2] as you can see in Fig 4.2. This is not a simple motif likely to have been created independently of Mlle Riego's books and I suspect that it was copied.

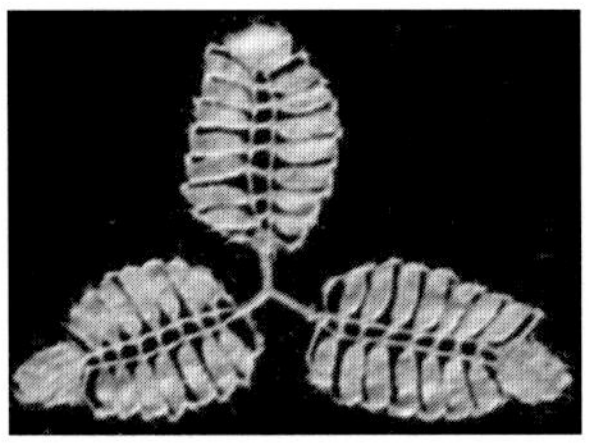

a

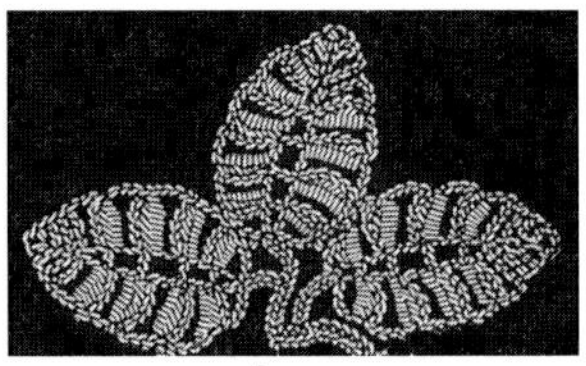

b

Library of the Author

Fig 4.2 Comparison of compound leaf motifs.
a Motif from the outer upper right of Fig 4.1.
b Motif from Mlle Riego's Crochet Collar with British Emblems[3].

Although this d'oyley resembles those of Mme Goubaud's, there is nothing to suggest a date – d'oyleys do not change much over time. Then I encountered another example which may well have been worked in the 1850s, or 1860s. We know that fall caps of this type were in fashion in 1853 as the Marslands Manual gave a pattern of this shape as shown in Fig 3.7, p. 13 of the companion volume, *Mademoiselle Riego and Irish Crochet Lace.* Keep in mind also that roses, thistles and shamrocks were used together in needlework designs of the 1850s.

I include a sketch of the outline of the fall cap in Fig 4.3 and the detail of a small section, as marked, in Fig 4.4. It is the only example I have seen with these motifs in a formal, rather than a random arrangement. It was worked in very fine thread with only a limited amount of ground.

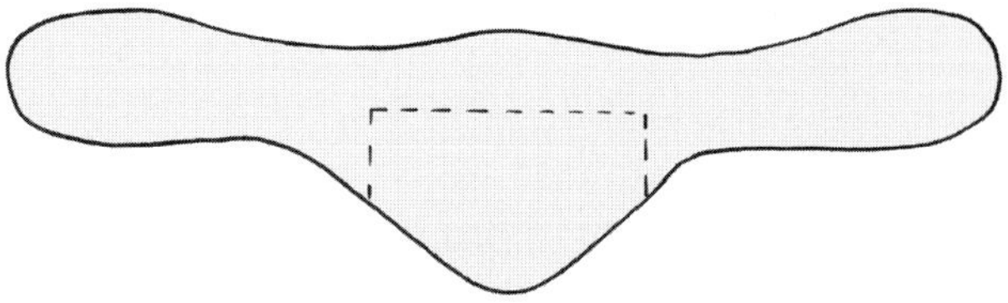

Fig 4.3 The outline of a fall cap with raised roses, thistles and shamrocks. Jeanette Moles (18 x 66 cm).

The close up below shows a raised rose at the base of the scallop with thistles either side. The triplets of shamrocks mid way up the sides have the thin triangular centre and simple leaflets in W. Carter's book, Fig 3.8, p. 26, also a few nondescript medallions. The tiny circles on crossed stems, which are also in Madame Goubaud's d'oyleys and in Fig 4.1, are also repeated in the unusual edge. These roses have more rows of petals and are tighter than those seen previously in this book.

Photograph taken by the Author

Fig 4.4 Detail of the fall cap, Fig 4.3.

I saw no lace in this uncommon style in museums or other collections in Ireland.

The History of the Raised Rose

The large d'oyley, Fig 4.1 and the fall cap, Fig 4.4, both include the raised rose which for many people is virtually the trademark of Irish crochet. No one has ever considered the history of this motif, which has several rows of petals arranged in a particular way, directly behind each other giving a raised, layered effect.

When was the raised rose first used?

In the earliest known report in 1853, John Maguire wrote of a bertha featuring roses with the petals raised in folds, in a collection of beautiful crochet designed and worked in the Ursuline Convent at Blackrock in Co. Cork[4], the earliest known source of Irish crochet. The crochet skills of the nuns probably came originally from Paris, p. 14. Perhaps they brought the raised rose with them.

Also in 1853, in her *Crochet Book Thirteenth Series*, Mlle Riego published the first pattern I have seen with this three-dimensional flower in her Collar à la Vallière', reproduced here as Fig 4.5[5]. It is a sophisticated design, and very different to her other work, although in the same year in *The Needle*, she also gave the same basic pattern arranged for a chemisette[6].

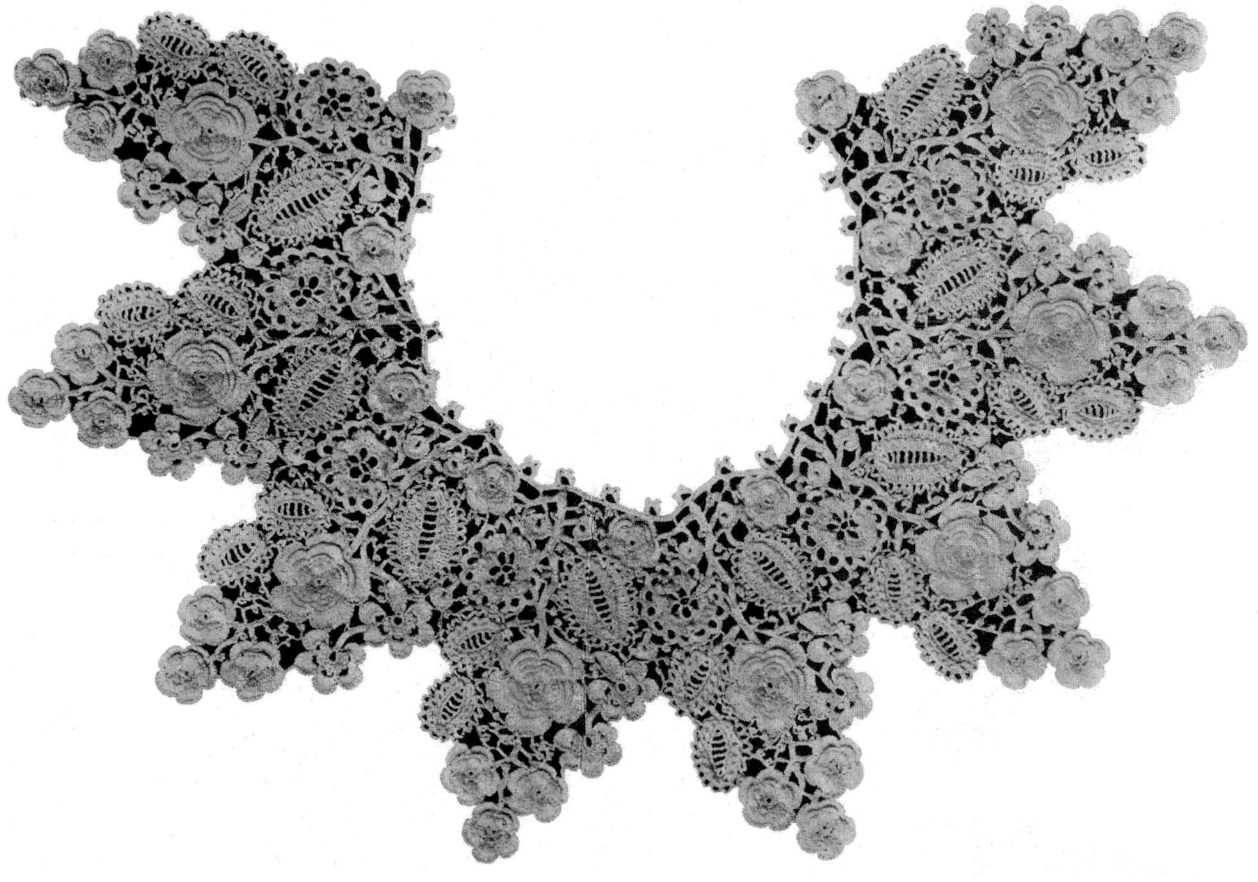

Library of the Author

Fig 4.5 Collar à la Vallière as given in Mary Card's Crochet Book No 3, Irish Crochet[7].

In 1854 or earlier, a somewhat similar rose was used in an early Irish crochet lapel in the collection of the Victoria & Albert Museum, p. 19.

In Mrs Meredith's book of 1865[8], Mary Desmond spoke of her crochet roses as life-like, so they may have had raised petals.

Mme Hardouin considered the raised rose to be an old motif[9].

What was the origin of the raised rose?

There is another French connection (in addition to the Ursuline nuns returning from Paris to their convent in Blackrock, p. 11). Mary Card said the pattern of the Collar à la Vallière, Fig 4.5, in her *Crochet Book No 3, Irish Crochet,* of 1916 was 'taken from a very old French crochet book, having quaint hand-drawn illustrations and published early in last century by Mlle Riego'. Mary Card acknowledged Mlle Riego as the designer and the wording of the pattern is almost identical to that in Mlle Riego's 1853 book[10]. Several other patterns in Mary's Irish crochet book so closely resemble those in Mme Hardouin's French books that I believe Mary had access to them along with other French books and crochet lace.

In one of Mlle Riego's letters recently discovered in the Cork City & County Archives[11], she said that she had published 76 books, which is more than the 70 titles I found[12]. Perhaps some of the books not accounted for were published in France.

Some English needle lace dating from the 1600s is another possible origin. I have in mind here the flower in needle lace in the collection of the Victoria & Albert Museum as shown in Fig 172 of Santina Levey's *History of Lace*[13]. It is very similar to the crochet raised rose. Copying the traditional needle and bobbin laces was, after all, the original basis of Irish crochet and many of Mlle Riego's designs.

Germany, which was a pioneer in publishing crochet books in the 1840s, is another possible source as Madame Ashton wrote of the idea of 'embossed' crochet being of German origin[14]. Esther Potter's bibliography[14] listed a German Raised Crochet Book, written by J.C.E.A, which I was unable to find.

As discussed in the companion volume, *Mademoiselle Riego and Irish Crochet Lace* the raised rose appears as mainstream, rather than 'Irish' crochet in the English pattern books from the 1870s[15]. It was also in early issues of the needlework magazines which are outside the scope of this book. Then, towards the end of the nineteenth century, the raised rose became the dominant feature of a new style of Irish crochet lace, shown in Chapter 7, p 46.

Part II
Revival of the Irish Lace Industry

Chapter 5
Alan Cole, James Brenan, the Schools of Art and the Convents

Even though huge numbers of people had emigrated, by the 1880s Ireland was still over-populated and under-employed. The decline of crocheting and lacemaking was unfortunate as these industries had often paid well and suited the women and girls living on farms.

In 1883, however, exhibitions in London and Cork brought together two remarkable civil servants who began a new era for the Irish laces. Alan Cole (1846–1934) was an expert on lace, embroidery and design at the Department of Science and Art in London. James Brenan RHA (c. 1837–1907), was an artist and Headmaster at the Cork School of Art. Brief biographies are given in Appendix III.

The publications of Alan Cole and James Brenan, along with Peter Murray's chapter in *Cork History and Society: Interdisciplinary Essays on the History of an Irish County*[1] and the website www.crawfordartgallery.com/1876-1900.html, give details of this revival in southern Ireland. The recently-discovered newspaper correspondence of Michael Holland of Cork provides another viewpoint[2].

Alan Cole described the situation in 1883[3]:

> The trade had become stagnant, the public being satiated with Irish laces. Stocks of poorly patterned goods of indifferent material were held by merchants. Prices had declined and the wages paid for labour had fallen. It seemed as if the lace industry in Ireland was irretrievably moribund. At this juncture a number of important firms who had dealt in Irish laces decided to make an effort to save the industry by holding an exhibition of Irish lace in Mansion House [London] in 1883. Every description of Irish lace and crochet work was then displayed.
>
> The cleverness of the different sorts of handicraft was generally acknowledged, but it was felt that the artistic or ornamental taste displayed in them was not only dull but was low in standard; and a few specially prepared specimens made from good patterns and with superior threads did not materially alter this feeling.

The exhibition awakened enough interest for a few Irish members of Parliament to ask the Department of Science and Art to give lectures on the making and designing of lace in Ireland. Limerick was the first centre to apply.

The Cork School of Art

When James Brenan visited the South Kensington Museum to ask for a loan for the 1883 Cork Industrial and Fine Art Exhibition, he arranged for Alan Cole to visit Cork[4].

Because the lecture and lantern show was delayed by a problem in darkening the room, the two men had time to walk together through the exhibition. They agreed that even though the lace was beautifully worked, it was marred by poor design and very bad drawing, just as it had been at the Mansion House Exhibition. Afterwards they wrote to the many convents that had exhibited, to offer classes in drawing and design and so began a long-term joint venture[5].

James Brenan was to visit each class once a month, inspect the work done by pupils and nuns, lecture, give directions as to the work for the ensuing month and generally guide their efforts. Convent women with some art education would be trained to take classes and work towards the Art Class Teacher's Certificate. This programme, approved by the Department of Science and Art at South Kensington, applied to all the Irish laces including Carrickmacross, Limerick (embroidered net laces), Kenmare, Youghal (needlepoint styles) and Irish crochet[6].

Alan Cole was active back in London, where he raised the large sum of £500 by public subscription for the Irish lace industry. He came over from England in 1885, 1889 and 1897 to advise and lecture[7]. His wife was on the committee of eminent people set up in 1884 to obtain new patterns [8].

During the first year 'the students practised freehand drawing from the flat and geometrical drawing'. In the second year 'they did model drawing, ornament from the cast and made working drawings from photographs of antique lace, correcting the form when necessary'. In the third year they drew plant forms from nature and designed patterns. Wherever possible the class was set up close to the workroom so that trial pieces could be made. Good specimens of antique lace bought with a grant from the Committee of the Cork Exhibition and the Department of Science and Art were lent to the convents every month[9].

Progress was rapid. By 1884 most of the eight classes at lacemaking centres and six similar ones at convents in southern Ireland included pattern-designing for various sorts of lace and embroidery and were in direct touch with groups of lacemakers. Dealers commissioned work from students in the small lace-designing classes at these schools. Seventy pounds of the money which Alan Cole had raised in London was used for prizes for lace design competitions, which were a feature of the South Kensington system[10].

There was one major problem. The Cork School of Art building was in such a poor state that at one time the students had to work under umbrellas[11]. James Brenan's commonsense, shrewdness and tact helped to persuade William Horatio Crawford, a local businessman and art lover, to donate £20,000 for the complete remodelling of the existing School and the construction of a new extension[12].

Library of the Author

Fig 5.1 The Crawford Municipal School of Art presented to the city of Cork by William Horatio Crawford in 1885.

The 1885 opening of this large, impressive building in 1885 was important enough for the Prince and Princess of Wales to attend. The outside of the building was decorated with flags and the entrance hall was laid with carpet. The Princess led the procession through the building, leaning on James Brenan's arm. Not everyone approved of the situation and the noise from the large crowd in the street completely drowned the men students cheering the Royal party and the women singing 'God Save the Queen'. The crowd hissed, cheered for Parnell and sang 'God Save Ireland'[13].

Two hundred and sixty eight students attended the School in 1887. James Brenan was very proud of the awards they won. There were by then seven branch classes in lace design affiliated with the School in Cork. Some were nearby, such as St Vincent's Convent, Cork and the Ursuline Convent, Blackrock. Others were a little further away at the Presentation Convent at Youghal, and the Convent of Mercy, Kinsale. Three were in the adjoining Co. Kerry at the Convents of the Poor Clares at Kenmare and the Presentation Convents at Killarney and Tralee[14]. Classes at Skibbereen in Co. Cork and further north at Thurles in Co. Tipperary soon followed [15].

The classes were so successful that by 1888 over 300 workers associated with the various lace classes in Co. Cork and Co. Kerry were 'earning a 'very decent and respectable livelihood' from their lace. Designs were being sold to major lace firms. The students continued to win many scholarships, medals and prizes[16]. Some examples of the designs appear in Chapter 7.

The good results extended into the south east. When Alan Cole visited the Carmelite Convent at New Ross in Co. Wexford in 1889 there was a good attendance of lacemakers and crochet workers despite very wet weather. When he visited three years before there were only about 40 workers and no young people. Significantly, the output of crochet and lace had increased since the introduction of new designs of Michael Holland, a student at the Cork School of Art and the supervisor for the crochet dealer Dwyer & Co[17].

When James Brenan left the Cork School of Art to become Headmaster of the Dublin Metropolitan School of Art (DMSA) early in 1889, there was a 'gloom over the entire establishment'. At his farewell several students praised his achievements and presented him with a service of plate and an address in the form of an illuminated album'[18].

The interest in crochet and lace was so great that the next year the new headmaster, Mr. W. Mulligan, arranged for crochet classes for the 'lady amateurs', who paid ten shillings a quarter whereas the 'bona fide' workers in the 'industrial class' paid only a half-crown (2/6)[19].

The Dublin Metropolitan School of Art

The special class for lace designing which James Brenan set up at the DMSA in 1890 was also a great success[20]. The students won many awards and the class needed more space by 1902. Designs were sold to the Hungarian government, Walpole's (retailers in Dublin), the Hibernian Lace Company, the Congested Districts Board and the Royal School of Art Needlework.

The Dublin course was similar to that in the south; the students studied the best antique pieces, learnt to make lace, took their 'motifs' from natural flowers, leaves and fruits and were encouraged to develop their own style[21]. Alice Jacob, an experienced teacher-designer, conducted the lace and embroidery classes there for many years. She also taught at the Cork School of Art and worked for the Lace Depot[22]. One of her Irish crochet designs appears on p. 45.

James Brenan also set up lace classes at Loreto Abbey, Rathfarnham and at the Dominican Convent in Cabra, Dublin for which the DMSA provided teachers until the sisters in these convents became approved teachers of art. The DMSA also had connections with classes at Crossmaglen in Co. Armagh, the Ursuline Convent at Thurles in Co. Tipperary, the Brigidine Convent in Co. Carlow and the Dominican convents at Dún Laoghaire in Co. Dublin and Co. Wicklow[23]. James Brenan visited the lacemaking schools and centres around Dublin[24].

The DMSA also became involved in primary education when, in July 1900, it began the first summer course in lace and embroidery for national school teachers[25].

When Alan Cole came across from London in 1885 and 1889 his visits were mainly to the southern areas of Ireland where there was a close network of lace schools, especially in the convents. In 1897 he also went to many out-of-the-way non-convent lace schools in the north, such as Clones in Co. Monaghan and Lisnaskea in nearby Co. Fermanagh. He delivered a lecture on the Irish Lace Industry in Londonderry[26]. Details of his delightful reports are in Chapter 6.

For at least fourteen years Alan Cole and James Brenan worked to improve the Irish laces, working within the South Kensington system administered by the Department of Science and Art in London. This system was criticised by J. W. Turpin in his history of the DMSA, but the shortcomings he pointed out, such as the lack of a higher intellectual level of study, did not seem to be a problem for the lace classes[27].

Criticisms of the South Kensington Initiatives for the Irish Crochet Lace Industry

Other criticisms of the South Kensington system were voiced in letters to the editor of various Irish papers. In the late 1890s Michael Holland (1855–1950), queried the claim that his improved crochet lace patterns were the result of his attendance at the Cork School of Art and of Alan Cole's comments on his designs[28].

In reply, Alan Cole criticised some of Michael Holland's designs. He also quoted an earlier letter of Mr. Holland's saying that he found Mr. Cole's help to be very valuable. Alan Cole conceded however, that designing for the trade was different to working for examinations. For example, a design that was artistically beautiful could be so time-consuming that it was not a commercial proposition[29].

Michael Holland was not the only critic. Alan Cole mentioned 'A Crochet Lace Manufacturer', another letter-writer who had unfavourable comments. The editor of the *Irish Textile Journal* ended the correspondence saying that until Mr. Cole came to Ireland, nothing had been done to improve the designs of Irish laces. The editor believed that great advances had been made.

In another letter, Alan Cole criticised Michael Holland's dealings with one of the convents who wanted to raise the standard of their crochet workers[30].

In letters to other papers, the *Freeman* and the *Month* in 1891, Michael Holland questioned the need for new designs, as over 50 pattern books containing designs for crochet had been available at the time[31]. He suggested that it made more sense to encourage designs for the trade to meet fashion than the competition designs done by students in the lace schools. He went on to claim that new patterns from amateurs and students, for which a committee had paid over £320, were considered for the most part, practically worthless.

He believed that it would have been better to encourage the existing centres of crochet and lace making rather than start new ones. He was supported by Mr. Montagu Griffin.

Michael Holland noted that the combined production (presumably of crochet) of the various convents under South Kensington direction for the previous six years would not equal the turnover of a single trader in one year before 1883, yet this trader (presumably his employer), was 'studiously ignored and insulted by officials' of the English Department of Science and Art. He believed that 'the scheme for promoting the art of lacemaking in Ireland by a committee at South Kensington had been an absolute failure'. He agreed with Mr. Griffin's suggestion that Ireland establish its own Science and Art Department.

Michael Holland's claims are supported by the substantial amount of good crochet mentioned in the official account of the 1883 Cork Exhibition (p.14). Dwyer & Co, his employer, was, in 1889, a large crochet dealer in Cork with a good reputation in the United States[32].

On the other hand, this was the exhibition where Alan Cole and James Brenan found a poor standard of design of lace. We have no illustrations from the Cork Exhibition, but the ones of the Cork crochet in the 1883 Mansion House Exhibition of Irish laces in London and in Ben Lindsey's 1886 book shown earlier in Figs 3.8, 3.9 and 3.11 are at least plainer and simpler than the Clones examples, Figs 2.1, 2.5, 2.6, 2.7, 3.1, 3.2, 3.3, and 3.4[33].

Alan Cole's leadership, his knowledge of lace and design, his position in the Department of Science and Art and his fund-raising in London played a vital role in the revival of the Irish laces. However his almost aggressive newspaper correspondence with Michael Holland along with his criticism of the Lace Depot designs and sale of his own patterns shows another side of his nature[34].

By way of contrast, James Brenan was a gentler man who was regarded with affection by his students, p. 34. His tact and diplomacy as headmaster attracted the important Crawford and Gibson bequests to the Cork School of Art[35]. He had a heavy work-load, not only of administration but of teaching on his regular visits to the lace classes. He made a substantial contribution to the revival of the Irish laces.

Further details of Michael Holland's life and crochet lace designing are in Chapter 7 and in my other book, *Mademoiselle Riego and Irish Crochet Lace*.

Chapter 6

Other Organizations and People Involved in the Revival

Many remarkable people and organizations were involved in the renascence of the Irish laces.

The literature sources for the developments in the northern areas were William Coyne's book on Ireland's agricultural and cultural industries, J. W. Turpin's history of the Metropolitan School of Art in Dublin, Alan Cole's report on his 1897 Irish visit, Elizabeth Boyle's history of Irish needlework, Máire Treanor's book with extensive oral history of Clones lace and Nellie Ó Cléirigh's account of the lives of Irish lace makers and Lady Aberdeen[1].

The main organizations involved were the Branchardière Fund, the Congested Districts Board, the Department of Agricultural and Technical Instruction, the general Irish education system, the Irish Industries Association, the Lace Depot and the Royal Dublin Society.

The two leading figures in this interconnected group of organizations were Ben Lindsey and Lady Aberdeen.

Ben Lindsey (1819–93)[2] was a lace dealer who in about 1868 established the Lace Depot, an attractive showcase and shop at 76 Grafton Street in Dublin which Lady Aberdeen bought about 20 years later [3]. Much of the history in the earlier chapters is based on his well-illustrated books on the history and origin of the Irish laces[4].

Lady Aberdeen (1857–1939), the wife of the Lord Lieutenant or Viceroy, the King's representative in Ireland (1886, 1906–1915), was very active in promoting Irish industries generally and the Irish laces in particular[5].

When she left Ireland at the end of her husband's short first term in 1886 she remained involved and personally chose the unpaid board of directors of the Lace Depot once she owned it[6].

An enthusiastic and capable organizer, Lady Aberdeen set up the Irish Industries Association (IAA) in the mid 1880s to develop and promote scattered industries, initially for the International Exhibition at Edinburgh in 1886[7]. Several years later the IAA administered the Branchardière Fund, which financed crochet and lace improvement projects p. 38.

She organized the ambitious exhibition of Irish goods at the Irish village in the Columbian Exhibition in Chicago in 1893, and the 40 Irish girls she took to demonstrate the various forms of lacemaking helped to make the Irish village a great success. Her close involvement made her aware of some of the subtleties of arranging such a venture. She noted, for example, that the men wanted to include the prettiest girls regardless of their lacemaking skills and that she needed to personally guarantee the safety of the girls[8]. However, other titled women played a role when Lady Aberdeen was no longer in Ireland. For example, Countess Cadogan organized the magnificent display of Irish manufacturers known as the Countess Cadogan's Textile Exposition held in Dublin in 1897[9]. Many years later Lady Aberdeen was involved again, being responsible for much of the Irish lace displayed and sold at the 1908 Franco-British Exhibition in London[10].

New Government Initiatives

The teaching of crochet improved greatly after the Congested Districts Board began classes in the poor and remote counties of Donegal, Sligo, Mayo, Kerry and a few parts of Cork in 1891. These were very suitable places as crochet lacemaking was a rural industry[11].

The Department of Agricultural and Technical Instruction which was set up several years later, in 1899, subsidized teachers and young industries. For example, they employed Mary Nagle at the St. Louis Convent at Clones for a few years and also paid Sister Mary Columba, probably at the Convent of Mercy at New Ross in Co. Wexford[12].

These lace and crochet classes were very successful. The teachers were responsible for obtaining the patterns and thread and selling the work as well as conducting the crochet lessons. They had a full programme, often with morning classes for adults and afternoon ones for children[13].

There were also classes in the convents, in the big municipal institutes in the general school system in eleven different counties and in private lace schools. Thousands of girls benefited, mostly the daughters of small farmers and labourers[14].

The list of organizations represented in the Home Industries Section of the Irish International Exhibition at Dublin in 1907 in Appendix IV gives some idea of how many different groups there were. A considerable number of these schools were probably also active in the late nineteenth century[15].

The Congested Districts Board teachers were often from around Clones. Their training, usually either at the Cork School of Art, the Lace Depot in Dublin, Commercial Art classes in the Metropolitan School of Art in Dublin or Congested Districts Board teacher classes in South Kensington, often included designing as well as in their particular form of needlework[16]. The crochet workers frequently created their own designs[17].

Going to the classes could be hard work. At Sneem in Co. Kerry, sixteen of the pupils in the evening class lived about five miles away so they had to walk close on ten miles a day for four months in the winter. One girl walked sixteen miles a day and attended on 72 of the 81 days of the class. Many of the girls helped on the farms, so their lace or crochet was worked part-time[18].

There were restrictions too. Girls needed to have reached their fourteenth birthday and were considered too old at seventeen. They were refused employment if their younger brothers and sisters did not attend school[19].

In some of the poorer homes, crochet was the only form of lacemaking possible, and the girls sometimes kept it clean by wrapping it up or putting it in their beds[20].

Small Non Government Organizations

The revival of the Irish laces in the north occurred later than in the south. Some northern convents were active, especially at Clones, the major centre of Irish crochet in the north, but the northern lace schools were often conducted by other organizations and charitable women (Appendix IV). For example, the Belfast Institute had classes in 1901[21] and Lady Brooke ran a school at Lisnaskea in Co. Fermanagh[22]. 'Very fine and special (crochet) work' came from Miss Fleming, a lace and crochet manufacturer at Park, Co Londonderry, in 1897[23].

We know a good deal about the revival around Clones from Alan Cole, from an English magazine in about 1901, and from the books of Elizabeth Boyle (1971) and Máire Treanor (2002). Crocheting was one of the major occupations in the 1901 census and was so well respected that girl babies were valued more than boys[24].

The sisters of the St. Louis Convent in Clones employed Miss Harris, Miss Mulligan, Miss Mary Nagle, Miss Tierney and Sister Roche to teach crochet and design. The convent supervised the work of the Co-operative Lace Society and provided a venue for its meetings[25]. (Details of some Clones women who taught for the Congested District Board are in Appendix V.)

Isabel Madden played a key role in the 1890s, supervising and obtaining orders[26]. When Alan Cole visited her group in 1897 he suggested that the motifs be simplified and arranged differently. He thought there were great opportunities for developing the Clones work if a proper supply of paper patterns could be arranged. He was saddened by the 'strong disinclination of the local workers to do more than repeat the forms and shapes they were used to and by their reluctance to take up the suggestions of eminent dealers who knew what the market wanted. There was a strong demand for their really good work but a glut of the poorer variety[27].

At the turn of the century Isabel Madden offered to have the Clones women complete the work of any amateurs who needed help with working the patterns provided in an Irish crochet issue of the English needlework magazine *Needlecraft Practical Journal*[28]. The readers could often work the motifs, but crocheting the background or ground was much more difficult. In addition Isabel Madden also supplied 'properly worked specimens' of the sprigs (motifs) for one shilling or upwards, according to the size (the 14-page magazine cost two pence). This was an enterprising move to keep the Clones women in work and promote Irish crochet.

Ben Lindsey helped to raise the standard of the Clones workers by providing market feedback and beautiful floral designs from the South Kensington Art Society[29].

Lady Aberdeen visited Clones in the 1880s and continued to take a personal interest in the crochet there even after she and her husband had left Ireland[30].

The Branchardière Trust Fund and the Royal Dublin Society

Other needs of the Irish crochet lace industry not covered by the government classes and private schools were sometimes met by the Branchardière Trust Fund set up at the beginning of the 1890s with a bequest from Mlle Eleonore Riego de la Branchardière, an English crochet and needlework designer. The £4,000 she left in her Will to assist the Irish lacemakers financed a range of projects, such as new designs, the prizes for the Royal Dublin Society (RDS) lace competitions and further training[31]. Further details of the Branchardière Fund are presented in the companion volume *Mademoiselle Riego and Irish Crochet Lace.*

Some of the Irish crochet designs entered in the prestigious 1899 RDS competition are shown in the next chapter, pp. 43 & 46. The RDS has a long history of fostering craft especially lacemaking[32] and still uses the Branchardière Fund for prize money for their Annual Crafts Competition. The Award of the RDS William Smith Perpetual Challenge Cup, the First Prize for Class 17.2 Lace, in 2005 to Kathie Earle's Irish Crochet Necklace is one of the latest in the tradition[33].

Marketing

The marketing of Irish crochet carried out by the Lace Depot and Cork dealers such as Michael Holland, Dwyer's and Lyons' was mentioned earlier (p. 14). Elizabeth Quigley set up as a dealer in Co. Mayo after she heard how much profit the Lace Depot made[34]. Other dealers are listed in trade directories now available on CD such as *Kenny's Irish Manufacturers Directory*[35].

Elizabeth Boyle and Máire Treanor write at length of the various outlets for Irish crochet. A few women had their personal contacts which they kept secret, even to the extent of going to another town to post their work, sometimes to America[36].

The Americans and the French were the largest buyers of the southern Irish crochet[37]. Tourists passing through Kenmare bought much of the local output in 1897[38]. The individual convents often made their own arrangements. Alan Cole wrote of the Carmelite Convent in New Ross sending orders to London and Paris[39].

It took many years but the good work of many dedicated people and organizations greatly improved the quality and quantity of the Irish laces from the mid 1880s until well into the twentieth century.

CHAPTER 7
The Development of Irish Crochet Lace Design in the Early Revival

Attractive designs in the latest fashions were vital for the lace market which by the mid 1880s had become very competitive. A selection of new professional Irish crochet lace designs is shown in this chapter, mostly connected with the Schools of Art and the competitions which were part of the South Kensington system.

Cork

Michael Holland

The best known commercial designer of Irish crochet lace was Michael Holland (1855–1950) who was foreman of the crochet workers employed by Dwyer's as well as a student at the Cork School of Art in the late 1880s and early 1890s. He spoke at James Brenan's farewell and won a prize two years later in 1891 so he was obviously respected and capable[1].

Alan Cole included three of Michael Holland's crochet designs in his 1888 book on the renascence of the Irish laces[2]. He also wrote in his 1889 trip report that Michael's very successful crochet lace designs were responsible for a great increase in the number of workers to 500[3]. The same designs also illustrated M. Lefébure's book on embroidery and lace which Alan Cole translated from the French and annotated in 1899[4].

In 1890 and 1891 Michael Holland and others questioned the value of the work Alan Cole and the Department of Science and Art in South Kensington had done for the Irish lace and crochet industries. This led to the publication of a series of letters in the pages of various Irish newspapers (p. 35).

Michael Holland left Dwyer's to set up his own business as a crochet dealer some time in the early 1900s and between 1904 and 1920 he supplied many of the big shops in Cork[5].

He was a personal friend of Mlle Riego, the talented and prolific English needlework designer[6]. I believe he was her collaborator when she attempted to promote Irish crochet in Ireland with her designs in about 1887. This intriguing story is told in the companion volume to this book, *Mademoiselle Riego and Irish Crochet Lace*. Further details of his long and varied life are in Appendix VI.

Six of the Irish crochet designs in the Michael Holland Collection of Irish crochet in the Cork Museum[7] and one from the Michael Holland Collection of documents in the Cork City & County Archives are shown in Figs 7.1–8.

This Reticella style border, Fig 7.1, was one of the designs in Alan Cole's small book on the Irish laces in 1888[8].

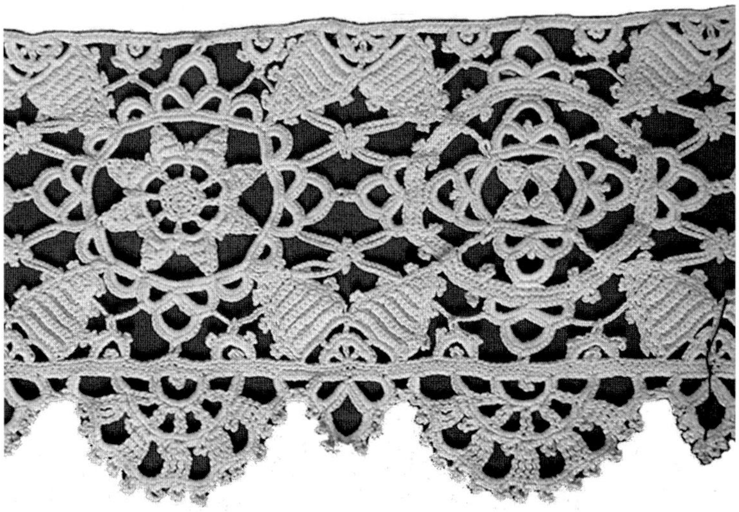

Photograph taken by the Author

Fig 7.1 A Michael Holland Reticella style border. 1883 Cork Museum, L1945.13 (9 cm deep).

The combination of what appear to be stylized thistles, leaves and grapes made of padded rings with only a minute central hole in Fig 7.2 is unusual. The ground is of paired bars with picots which were a feature in crochet in the 1870s and 1880s[9]. The elaborate edge features the padded rings used in the grapes and as filler motifs.

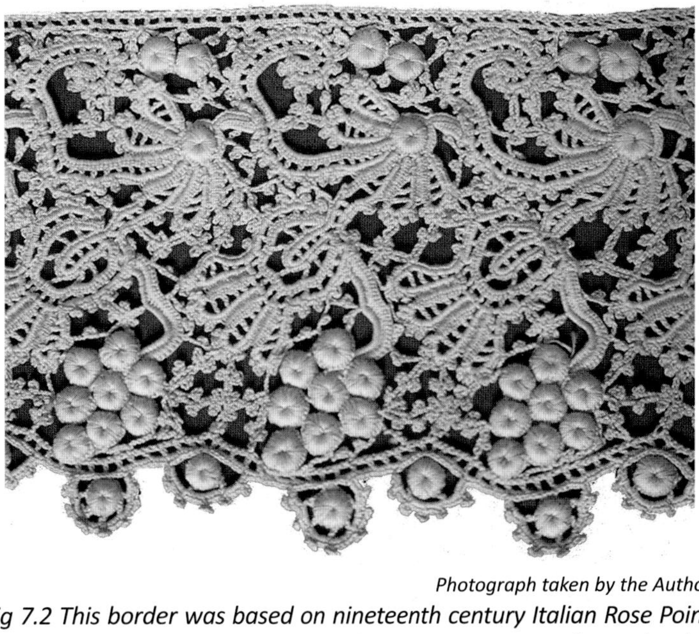

Photograph taken by the Author

Fig 7.2 This border was based on nineteenth century Italian Rose Point and was created in about 1900. Cork Museum, L1945.17 (9 cm deep).

A very fine ornate scalloped cuff, Fig 7.3 has stylized flowers and leaves, padded rings and scrolls.

Photograph taken by the Author

Fig 7.3 Another Michael Holland design in the Cork Museum, made in about 1896 L1945.14 (12 cm deep).

The close up of the cuff below in Fig 7.4 shows Clones knots on the surface of the scrolls and on the edge. The needle lace ground has a central tiny ring with single strands of thread joining the motifs.

Photograph taken by the Author

Fig 7.4 The detail of the cuff in Fig 7.3.

This attractive insertion, Fig 7.5, has solid curved motifs joined in some places by single threads, presumably made with a needle and in others by heavy crochet bars with a group of four picots at the joins. Michael Holland often used single threads in the ground. This design is quite different to any other Irish crochet lace seen up to this point and has a classical simplicity. Like the other laces in this Collection it is beautifully worked and I am tempted to pick up a crochet hook to recreate it. There is no information about when it was designed.

This is the first insertion to be included in the book. Borders and insertions often came in matching pairs and two examples of such sets designed by Michael Holland are shown in other books[10].

Photograph taken by the Author

Fig 7.5 An insertion designed by Michael Holland. Cork Museum, L1945.16 (6 cm deep).

The collar of medallions, shown below, is a particularly simple design of Michael Holland.

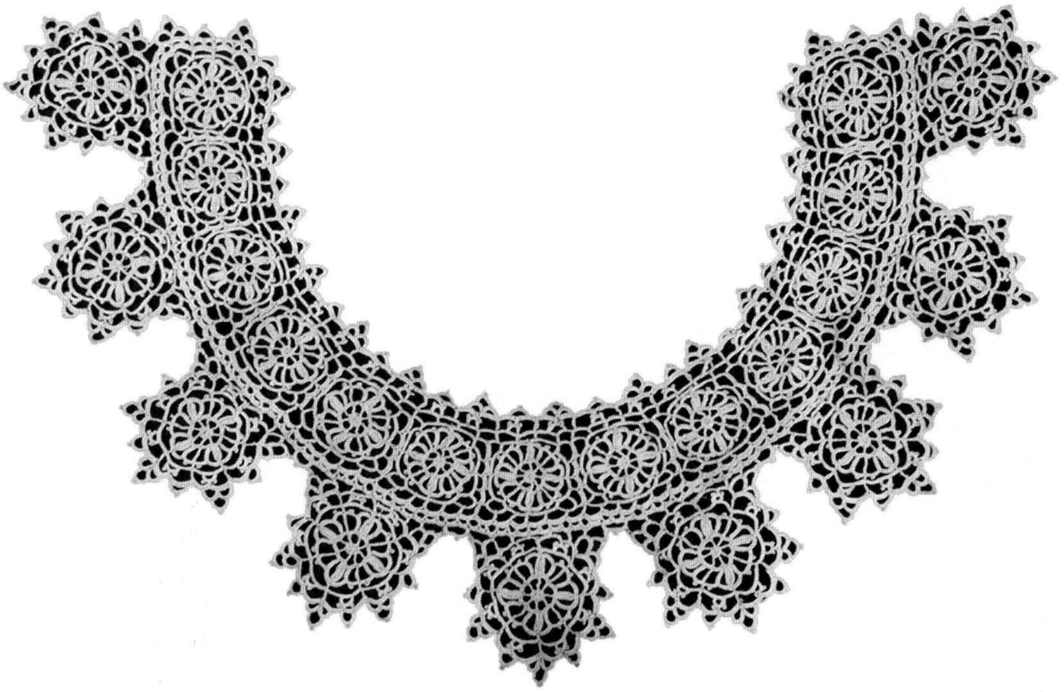

Cork Museum

Fig 7.6 A Michael Holland collar based on Genoese lace. 1883 Cork Museum, L1945.11 (32 x 20 cm).

This large, elaborate collar, Fig 7.7 has motifs used in the body of the design repeated in the neckline.

Cork Museum

Fig 7.7. A collar designed by Michael Holland. c.1900, L1945.20 (53 x 36 cm)

The Michael Holland Collection in the Cork City & County Archives has illustrations of eight borders and insertions, including the reticella style lace in Fig 7.1, three apparently based on Mlle Riego's Royal Jubilee Lace[11] and others in a somewhat similar style to Fig 7.8.

One of these, Fig 7.8, features stylized flowers and scrolls in a fine ground with large picots which are repeated along the lower edge.

Cork City & County Archives

Fig 7.8 A sophisticated border designed by Michael Holland. Cork City & County Archives.

Other Designers from Co. Cork

Minnie Nagle of the Cork School of Art designed a collar, Fig 7.9, which appeared in *Weldon's Practical Crochet*[12]. Weldon's must have been very pleased to have the pattern, as it is the only time they gave the name of the designer.

Library of the Author

Fig 7.9 A portion of a silk collar designed by Minnie Nagle in about 1901.

Many of the other designs illustrated in this chapter have connections with Alan Cole and/or James Brenan in Cork and Dublin. A particularly interesting group, Figs 7.10, 7.11 and 7.16 come from the *Scrapbook of the Royal Dublin Society Lace Competition for 1899*, a very valuable record of this important annual event. The designers were often mentioned in records of the Cork School of Art [13] and their details are included in Appendix VII.

The collars and borders were elaborate. The motifs included flowers, thistles, shamrocks, scrolls, hearts, cornucopias and padded rings, sometimes used singly, in crescents or in circles.

In addition to the usual ground of simple intersecting picot loops, there were heavy bars, clusters of picots, and what are probably Clones knots and Solomon's knots[14]. The use of several different grounds in the one piece was common practice and enhanced the design. There did not appear to be raised roses in any of the work. Note that many of the entries were only partly crocheted as it was after all, a design competition.

The only award made for crochet in this competition was given to the collar in Fig 7.10.

Royal Dublin Society

Fig 7.10 Georgina McKinlay's prize-winning Irish crochet collar in the 1899 RDS competition.

Royal Dublin Society

Fig 7.11 Emily Wilkinson entered this large collar in the RDS competition in 1899.

Amy Whitelegge of the Cork School of Art produced this elaborate design, Fig 7.12, which used flowers, scrolls, cornucopias and a heart, set in different grounds, some simple and others intricate[15].

Library of the Author

Fig 7.12 This Crochet Panel for Dress' was designed by Amy Whitelegge about the turn of the century and .illustrated James Brenan's chapter on Modern Irish lace in 1902[15].

This magnificent collar in Cork crochet, Fig 7.13, from an unnamed designer, has a wide array of stylized floral motifs in a sparse complex ground and an unusual edge of flowers on paired picot bars.

Library of the Author

Fig 7.13 A collar in Cork crochet which appeared in James Brenan's book chapter in 1902[15].

Crochet historians may care to look up other examples of the work of other unnamed Cork designers in Alan Cole's book *Irish Lace*, of 1902[16] and the superb collar on the cover of Ena Maidens' book *Technique of Irish Crochet Lace*[17]. There are some fine examples from the Presentation Convent at Youghal in Irish museums and in other books[18].

The Cork designs tended to be more open with larger motifs than the northern work[19] and were sometimes adventurous with new motifs rather than the traditional grotesque ones. The Clones crochet which is considered on p. 46 was said to be closer[20] and appeared to be more conservative.

Limerick/London

One of the earliest winners of prizes for crochet designs was Michael Hayes from Limerick who was a National Scholar at the National Art Training School, South Kensington.

In 1885 he was awarded fourteen of the twenty prizes which involved crochet, from the fund set up by Alan Cole in London. Michael Hayes dominated the field as the five laces selected for trial working included four of his designs yet no illustrations of them are known[21].

New Ross, Co. Wexford

Borders designed and worked at the Carmelite Convent, New Ross at the time of the revival include grotesque motifs seen in earlier chapters, as well as flowers and shamrocks. They have one of the traditional looped edges.

Called Modern crochet lace, Fig 7.14, this border is one of a series with a shamrock edge and ground with clusters of Clones knots[22].

Library of the Author

Fig 7.14 Modern crochet lace from the Carmelite Convent, New Ross.

Another border, Fig 7.15 also has grotesque motifs with a variety of fillings and in a complex ground with clusters of Clones knots.

V&AImages/Victoria & Albert Museum

Fig 7.15 Irish crochet from an unknown designer at the Carmelite Convent, New Ross, Circ. 537 1913.

I found no details of the designer(s) of the New Ross borders, but Alan Cole mentioned two in that area, Mr. S. J. Murphy, the Master of the Waterford School of Art[23] and Miss Dobbyn, who trained at that school[24].

Dublin

The Dublin entrants in the RDS competition were probably from James Brenan's lace design classes begun ten years earlier[25] and their work is in a very different style, Fig 7.16.

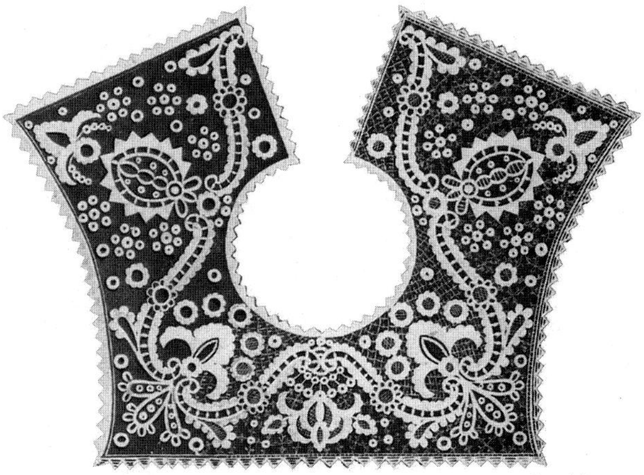

Royal Dublin Society

Fig 7.16 This collar was submitted by Miss F. M. White of Dublin to the 1899 RDS Lace Competition[26].

The imposing collarette, Fig 7.17, is the work of Alice Jacobs (p. 35), the highly-regarded designer-teacher at the Metropolitan School of Art in Dublin[27].

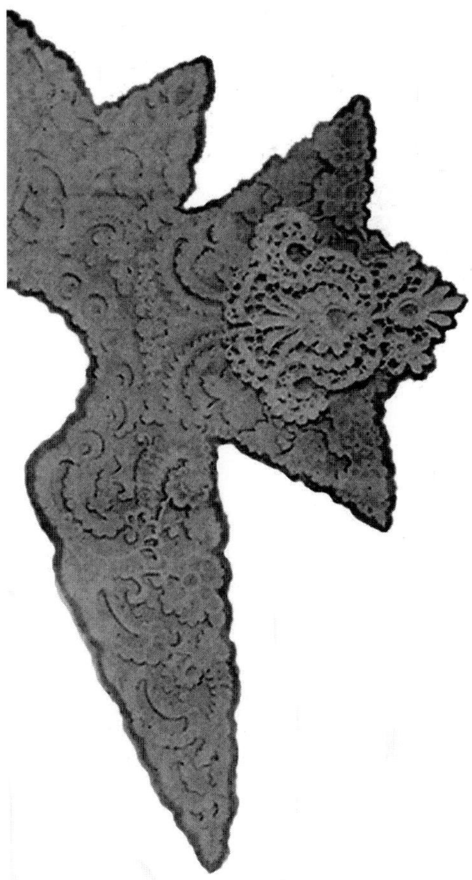

Library of the Author

Fig 7.17 An Irish crochet design by Alice Jacobs which illustrated a book chapter by James Brenan in 1902.

Clones and Surrounding Areas

The designs from the Lace Depot and the South Kensington Art Society used at Clones at one stage were mentioned earlier, p. 38 [28]. An influence from the south came to Clones with Miss Harris and Mary Nagle, who had trained at the Cork School of Art, pp. 38 & 53 [29].

I did not find any dated examples of professional designs from Clones in the 1880s and 1890s, although further research may locate some from this major centre of Irish crochet. Two beautiful pieces which are said to be old are shown in books by Irish crocheters from Clones. One is an elaborate collar of old Clones lace in silk on p. 17 of *Irish Crochet Lace* by the late Eithne d'Arcy[30] and the other is a dress piece with a shamrock Clones knot ground, at the centre front of the illustration on p. 75 of Máire Treanor's *Clones Lace: the Story of an Irish Crochet* [31]. This was made by an old woman who lived up in the hills of Fermanagh, the next county, was acquired by Eithne d'Arcy and is now in the collection of Máire Treanor.

James Brenan described the Clones work as very beautiful with a distinctive character. He believed it was capable of great development[32]. As mentioned earlier, p. 44, the Clones crochet was said to be closer and appeared to be more conservative.

It would appear that the fine trellis work, with raised roses and shamrocks in the centre of medallions, began around Roslea, Co. Fermanagh near Clones, although we do not know who led this development[33].

The trellis work became more fashionable at the turn of the century and replaced the older heavy work as the secrets and art of making and joining motifs died out around Clones[34]. The medallions were usually square, with a raised rose or shamrock at the centre, surrounded by picot loops and shells as seen in the earlier Guipure styles, p. 17, Fig 7.18.

Collection of the Author

Fig 7.18 Collar of trellis work. Author's collection, B811 (45 x 33 cm)

These medallions, which were made to a regular pattern, are easier to work than the older style which involved joining the motifs with a crochet background or ground. Nevertheless, as shown in Fig 7.19, some adjustments had to be made to produce the curves needed for most garments. Medallions of slightly different sizes and shapes were used, some extra picot mesh may be worked in between some units and the outer row has an extra medallion added to produce the arc.

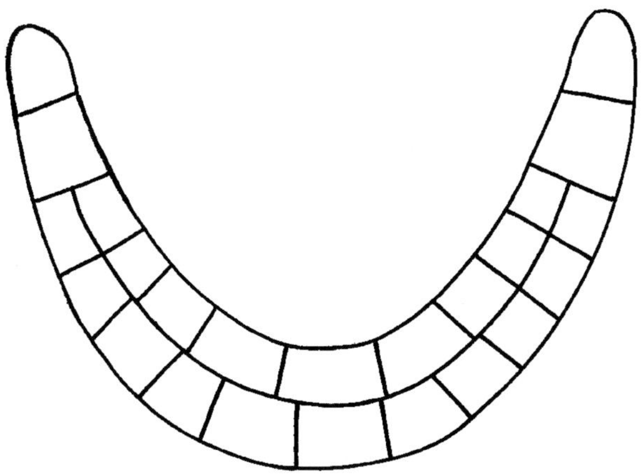

Fig 7.19 Diagram showing the shapes and arrangement of the medallions in the collar in Fig 7.18.

This trellis work was very dainty. It was eminently suited to the Edwardian fashions and was extensively used in a wide range of garments, accessories and household linen.

A few lace merchants had considerable influence on the work that was produced at this time. Ben Lindsey of Dublin has already been mentioned as providing designs, p. 38, for the Clones workers. Haywards, lace merchants of London began Royal Irish Guipure, a sumptuous style worked in silk in the 1880s[35].

To sum up

When I reflect back on the extensive amount of Irish crochet lace I have seen (Appendix VIII), I believe that the professional designers had an effect on the commercial work, both in the motifs used and the overall design. This is despite the fact that the crocheters often created their own designs and typically lived in remote areas[36]. No examples of this influence are presented here as it opens up a large field outside the scope of this book. I have only covered a few of the earlier styles and a selection of those in the revival. There is a wealth of material yet to be explored.

The long list of the centres which submitted Irish crochet lace to the Home Industries Exhibition in 1907, as detailed in Appendix V shows that there was indeed a large trade in Irish crochet lace.

Some of Michael Holland's early designs were very successful commercially, but we do not know which ones these were. Even though there are a number of examples of his work in books, archives, in the Cork Museum and the Victoria & Albert Museum, few of them are simple enough to suit the mass market (Figs 7.2, 7.3, 7.5 and two rose edgings not shown here are quite straightforward). The ones included in this book probably represent the best of his work as it is usually the finest and most attractive that is photographed and kept for museums.

The work which illustrates this chapter gives some idea of the beautiful lace which skilled crocheters with good designs can produce. The Irish crocheters were leaders in exploring and developing the craft.

The early Irish crochet lace was based on the needle and bobbin laces and then developed as an art form in its own right. For this reason, as well as the large number of schools, there is a great variety of styles, greater than most people realize. In the introduction to this book, p. 8, I explained the features which distinguish Irish crochet from mainstream crochet. These included two techniques, firstly working over cord and secondly, tacking the motifs worked separately onto a foundation pattern and then adding the background or ground. Another diagnostic feature was the use of shamrocks and raised roses.

However, some of the styles worked in the early days do not fit these guidelines. I refer particularly to the Lifted Guipure lace, p. 17, the Reticella style p. 24, the Plain Crochet Cork Fig 3.11, p. 26; and in later times Michael Holland's medallion collar, Fig 7.3, p. 41. It would appear that another category is needed, of laces which have an established history of being worked in Ireland.

The influence of Mlle Riego and the other English designers on Irish crochet appears to have been limited[37] and indeed towards the end of the century it was the Irish crochet which was leading the way in the English magazines.

Irish crochet lace did more than adorn women and their homes. It provided a vital source of income for many families, enabling them to survive the famine and later raise themselves out of poverty. It also gave the women dignity and freedom to use their imagination and be creative, which was rarely possible in the other laces. It is a significant part of the Irish heritage.

I hope that this book will tempt people to look more closely at the great variety of the lace in museums and private collections, along with the literature and portraits.

Appendix I

John Maguire, Mrs Susanna Meredith, Mrs Martha Roberts and Rev Walter Cramer Roberts

John Frances Maguire (1815–72) was a capable man of wide interests and a prolific writer. One of his earliest ventures was founding the *Cork Examiner* in 1841 to support Daniel O'Connell and the Repeal movement. He was called to the Bar in 1843 and after entering politics in 1852 represented Dungarvan from 1852–65 and then Cork for the rest of his life. He was also Lord Mayor of Cork for four years (1852, 1862–3 and 1864). On three occasions he visited Pope Pius IX, who made him a Knight Commander of St Gregory.

His publications include:

The Industrial Movement in Ireland as Illustrated by the National Exhibition of 1852, 1853.

'Limerick Lace', History of the Industry in "Industrial Movement in Ireland" 1852–3 ... Irish Quarterly Review 3, 1853, p. 771[1].

Removal of Irish Poor from England and Scotland: Shewing the Nature of the Law of Removal, the Mode in which it is Administered, the Hardships which it Inflicts, and the Necessity for Its Absolute and Unconditional Repeal (1854)

Curran; in the Senate and at the Bar (1856)

Rome and its Rulers (1856),

The Life of Father Mathew (1861)

The Irish in America (1866)

The Pontification of Pius IX (1870)

The Next Generation (3 volumes, 1871)

Home Government for Ireland; being a series of articles reprinted from *The Cork Examiner*, 1872[2].

Mrs. Susanna Meredith (1823–1901) was the daughter of the 'humane and enlightened' Governor Lloyd of the Cork County Gaol who developed work programmes for the inmates[3].

She married a young doctor at the age of about seventeen and began the Adelaide Lace School shortly after she was widowed in 1847. After the school closed in 1859 and her father died, she moved to London where she edited *The Alexandra*, a journal which promoted women's rights and employment, and wrote her book, *The Lacemakers*. The rest of her life was largely devoted to assisting women convicts and their children. Her evidence before the Gladstone Committee brought about prison reform. She provided sheltered accommodation and employment for many women on their release. In 1871 she established a village home for the children of convicted criminals at Addlestone, Surrey where she died in 1901.

Her other publications include:

The Sixth Work, or the Charity of Moral Effort (1866)

Wanted, Deaconesses for the Service of the Church (1872)

A Book About Criminals (1881)

Saved Rahab! (1881)

A biography, *Susanna Meredith: a Record of a Vigorous Life,* was written by Mary Anne Lloyd (1903)[4].

Martha C or Marsha Roberts was born in England in Middlesex, in about 1801. Her daughter, Amy C. was born in about 1834 and her son, Clayton C. in about 1836[5]. It is not clear where she taught in Co. Kildare; Susanna Meredith said Kilcullen and Ben Lindsey said Thornton which does not exist on the usual modern maps[6]. Máire Treanor[7] writes of her at Thornton House.

Ben Lindsey gives her husband's initials as W. C. and church records show that Rev. Walter Cramer was born in Co. Kildare in about 1802. He was educated at Eton College and Trinity College, Dublin. He graduated with a B.A. in 1824, followed by an M.A. in 1832, was ordained a deacon in the Church of Ireland in 1835 and served at Ballinafagh in Dublin from 1830 until 1938[8].

In 1848 the Rev Roberts left the Church of Ireland to work for the Church of England at Edwardstone in Suffolk where he remained until 1870[9]. Mrs Roberts referred to being in Co. Kildare when she wrote the letter which Mrs Meredith quoted in *The Lacemakers* in 1865[10].

A Mrs Cramer Roberts lent lace for the 1883 Mansion House Exhibition in London[11]. By this time if Mrs Roberts was still living, she would have been more than 80 years old so this lace may have come from a relative.

Appendix II

Entries with Crochet and Other Selected Garments in the 1853 Dublin Exhibition[1]

753 J.L. Barber & Co, Norwich, Manufacturer, sewing and crochet threads; registered designs by Hornsby for diamond netting or crochet; collars, sleeves, berthes & c. worked in the Irish Industrial Schools with Barber & Co's prize crochet thread.

758 W. Brittain, 5 Montpelier Hill, Dublin, two crochet quilts.

767 M. Canning, Rockville, Malin, [Co.Donegal], needle and crochet work, comprising basket covers, doyleys, trimmings & c. by girls at Malin.

770 E. Clarke, Deepham, Wynondham, Norwich, proprietor, crochet and pointwork collars, in imitation of Honiton and old marguerite guipure lace.

776 H.D. Constable, 3 Anne St, Clonmel, Co. Tipperary, designer, specimens of crochet work.

781 C .M. Davis, 60 Waterloo Rd, Dublin, designer, lace curtains with border of crochet work

782 The Misses Deane, Dundanion, Cork, specimens of crochet.

788 Adare Industrial Schools, Co. Limerick, Countess of Dunraven, patroness, ... a pair of crochet lace sleeves....

793 Miss E. Erskine, Harristown, Ardee, Co. Louth, specimens of Irish point lace (this may be crochet)

802 Harriet A Gray, 17 Prompton Crescent, near London, designer, a piece of fine crochet work.

806 Dora J. Gubbins, The Glebe, Ballingarry, Co. Limerick, specimens of ... crochet ... .

807 J. J. Hall, 7 High Street, Deptford, Kent, Crochet cover in cotton for back of sofa.

909 Miss E. Hallowell, 3 Lr Hartstonge St, Co. Limerick, ... horse's ear net done in crochet work

809 Miss [sic] C. Hand, Rectory Monaghan, Co. Monaghan, prod, specimens of work in crochet guipure, produced for charitable purposes.

814 Miss Maria Hunt, Killashee, Co. a vase of flowers in crochet.

819 Ladies' Industrial Society for Ireland, 76 Grafton St, Dublin, specimens of ... Spanish point lace, crochet, guipure... from schools in the counties of Kildare, Wexford and Fermanagh.

821 Adelaide Industrial School, 8 Duncan St, Cork, Crochet and other ornamental needle work

834 M. Louth, 112 Cork St, Dublin, quilt in crochet work.

838 Mrs Maclean, Rectory, Tynan, Co. Armagh, specimens of guipure and Irish point lace

839 Miss A. McGrath, Clifton Lodge, Blackrock, near Dublin, ottoman cover, in crochet work.

840 Miss S. McDowell, 9 Joy St, Belfast, Irish point lace head dress, collars and lappets, real point lace berthe, collars and lappet, handkerchief & c. of appliqué.

843 Miss McNaughton, 2 Hanover St, Edinburgh, cotton bed covers, worked in crochet.

848 Miss Montgomery, Benvarden, Ballymoney, Co. Antrim, proprietor, crochet work in imitation of Brussels lace and guipure; specimens of crochet insertions and edgings & c.

853 Miss G. Osborne, Kingstown , near Dublin, designer, dahlia and flower mats of crochet work.

857 Mrs M. Purcell, Halverstown, Kilcullen, Co. Kildare, proprietor, Spanish point lace, wrought at Halverstown school, ...

863 Mrs Ryan, Inch House, Borrisoleigh, Co. Tipperary, infants's cap and robe in finest crochet point. Openwork berthe, caps, collars and sleeves & c. in crochet guipure.

868 The Sisters of Mercy, Lower Baggot St, Dublin, ... double point crochet berthe, lappets sleeves & c. The work of the children of the industrial school of the Sisters of Mercy.

869 Sisters of Mercy, Kinsale, Co. Cork, Irish point lace, crochet.

879 Todd, Burns & Co, 47 Mary St, Dublin, proprietor, ... Irish needlework and crochet lace.

Appendix III
Alan S. Cole and James Brenan

Alan Summerly Cole (1846–1934) was an authority on a wide range of art, textiles and design at the Department of Science and Art, South Kensington[1]. He was the son of Sir Henry Cole, the larger-than-life cultural entrepreneur and civil servant who among other things was the founder and director of the South Kensington Museum, later renamed the Victoria & Albert Museum[2], but otherwise we have no information on his early life.

Alan Cole catalogued lace for museums at Cork, Dublin, Nottingham and South Kensington as well as a private collection. He also reported on the Honiton lace industry in 1887[3] and the Northampton, Buckinghamshire, and Bedfordshire lace industries in 1891[4]. He had overseas experience and reported on a French decorative arts exposition in 1882. He was a judge for a number of exhibitions, such as the International Lace Exhibition in 1874[5]

A few of his publications are listed in the references and bibliography; others, including some on embroidery, tapestry and paintings, may be found in the National Art Library catalogue at the Victoria & Albert Museum and in the bibliography given by Gertrude Whiting in *A Lace Guide for Makers and Collectors* of 1920[6]. His initials, ASC, are at the end of the scholarly 11-page entry on lace in the 1910–1911 edition of the *Encyclopaedia Britannica*[7]

James Brenan RHA (Royal Hibernian Academy) (c. 1837–1907) was a key figure in late nineteenth-century Irish art education[8] .

He was born in Dublin and trained to be an art teacher at the School of Art in Leinster House, the RHA School, and the Royal Dublin Society Drawing School. He also learnt in the studios of Owen Jones and Sir Matthew Digby Wyatt in London when he worked on the decoration of the Crystal Palace, London. In 1857, at the age of 20, he was appointed Assistant Master at the Birmingham School of Art. He studied for another three years at the training college at South Kensington with some occasional teaching in charge of art schools at Liverpool, Taunton and Yarmouth[9].

He became Headmaster at the Cork School of Art in 1860 at the age of 23, when there was a leadership crisis. He was very much respected by the students. The large donations he attracted for the Cork School of Art were of great value in its development. He was on the Executive Committee of the Cork Industrial and Fine Art Exhibition. He was a man of vision and thought along the same lines as John Ruskin and William Morris. He had overseas experience from visits to lace schools in France and Belgium and to schools of art in Hamburg, Stockholm, Berlin and Vienna[10]. Some of his publications are listed in the references and bibliography on pages .

In 1889, after 29 years at Cork, James Brenan moved to become Headmaster at the Metropolitan School of Art in Dublin. He retired in 1904 and spent the rest of his life in the Dublin suburb of Rathmines. His work with the Irish laces was only part of his legacy as he was one of the most influential and respected painters of his time, exhibiting a total of 107 paintings at the RHA[11]. (He should not be confused with another older painter, James Butler Brenan 1825–1889)[12].

James Brenan trained and worked within the South Kensington system which has come under fire both for its policies on art education in general[13] and for its efforts in improving Irish crochet lace designs in particular, pp. 33-5. The criticism seems to have been directed to Alan Cole and I found no adverse comment on James Brenan either personally or professionally.

Appendix IV

Organizations Represented in the Home Industries Section, Irish International Exhibition, Dublin 1907 which included Crochet[1]

Name	Address	No of hands
Co. Carlow		
Corris Cottage Industry	Bagenaltown	3
Co. Cavan		
Convent of Poor Clares	Ballyjamesduff	34
Convent of Mercy	Cootehill	(12)
Co. Cork		
Co Cork Industrial Association,	22 South Mall Cork	-
Blarney Crochet Cottage Industry	St Ann's Hill,	25
Convent of Mercy	Queenstown	(60)*
St. Joseph's Convent School	Kinsale	(140)
Youghal Co-operative Lace Society,Youghal	Youghal	(500)
St. Joseph's Technical School, Convent of Mercy	Bantry	(30)
South Presentation Convent	Douglas St, Cork	(58)
Lace Class, Crawford Municipal Technical Institute	Emmet Place, Cork	(65)
Co. Donegal		
Co. Donegal Joint Technical Instruction Committee		
Falcarragh Lace Class	Falcarragh	(30)
Lace and Crochet Class, St Louis Convent	Bundoran	(100)
Ballyshannon Lace School		84
Ballybofey Crochet Class		40
Letterkenny Crochet Class		39
Lace Class	Ardara	?
Co. Down		
Strangford Lough Industry	Oldcourt, Strangford	(85)
Co. Dublin		
Crochet School Sisters of Charity	Howth	24
Royal Irish Industries Association	76 Grafton St. Dublin	-
Co. Fermanagh		
Fermanagh Co. Committee of Ag. And Tech.Instr		
Countess of Erne's Home Industry	Derrylin, Belturbet	50
Letterbreen Lace Class		60
Tempo Crochet Class		50
Cooneen Crochet Class	Fivemiletown	6
Moan's Cross Crochet Class	Brookeboro'	40
Coa Crochet class	Ballinamallard	27
Brookeboro' Home Industries		78
Irish Lace School, Convent of Mercy	Enniskillen	(50)
Co. Galway		
Lace Class	Spiddal	?
Lace Class	Carna	?
Co. Kilkenny		
Innistiogue Cottage Industry	Innistiogue	25

Co. Kerry		
Presentation Convent	Tralee	13
Presentation Convent	Cahirciveen	(50)
Co. Longford		
McGooey Institute	Longford	(50)
Co. Lietrim		
Crochet Industry, The Convent	Manorhamilton	60
Co. Louth		
Lace Department of Mercy	Dundalk	(39)
Glogher Head Lace Industry	Clogher Head	40
Co. Mayo		
Convent of Mercy	Westport	50
Convent of Mercy	Castlebar	25
Convent of Mercy	Swinford	(12)
St Louis Convent	Kiltimagh	?
Lace Class	Pullathomas	?
Lace Class	Doohoma, Feesala	?
Lace Class	Kerry Park	?
Lace Class	Dereenda-derg	?
Lace Class	Tourmakeady	?
Co. Meath		
Co Meath Home Industries Society	The Depot, Navan	(100)
Co. Monaghan		
Convent of St. Louis	Clones	15
Collective Exhibit of Lace & Crochet organized by P.Kieran	Ulster Arms	400
Co. Laois (Queens County)		
	Ballinakill	-
Co. Roscommon		
Tisara Co-operative H. I. Society		35
Co. Sligo		
Sisters of Charity	Benada Abbey, Tubbercurry	(200)
Lace Class	Cliffoney	?
Co. Tipperary		
Sisters of Charity	Morton St, Clonmel	33
Co. Tyrone		
Lissan Co-operative Home Industries Society, Ltd	Lissan, Cookstown	40
Co. Westmeath		
Convent of Mercy	Moate	25

* Crochet was only one of the laces made here.

Appendix V

Clones Women Who Taught Crochet for the Congested Districts Board

The Congested Districts Board enticed some of the best Irish crochet lacemakers from the Clones area to go as 'missionaries' to the west of the country. These included Misses O'Connor and Tierney and three of the Cosgrove sisters. In 1897 Miss Tierney was at Ardara in Co. Donegal in 1902, Catherine Cosgrove went to Cliffoney in Co. Sligo, Margaret went to Roundstone in Co. Galway and Mary Jane to Renvyle in Co. Mayo[1].

Liza Gun from the nearby Derrylin, Co. Fermanagh went first to Bellmullet, Co. Mayo and then to Bruckless, Co. Donegal in the late 1890s where she founded a lacemaking school. Bruckless developed as a great centre for Irish crochet and sprigging work.

Elizabeth Quigley from Roslea, Co. Fermanagh near Clones trained as a lace teacher with the Lace Depot in Dublin then set up her first crochet school in Blacksod Bay on the coast of Co. Mayo. After Maud Gonne, an Irish revolutionary leader, told her how much profit the Lace Depot made on Irish crochet, Elizabeth set up as a lace dealer herself and paid the workers more[2].

Appendix VI

Michael Holland

Michael Holland was born at Clonakilty, Co. Cork in 1855 and the family later moved to Cork[1].

The first reference in his adult life comes in 1885 when he entered crochet work, No 521, in the Irish Artisans Exhibition in Dublin, in his position as honorary secretary of the Local Committee[2].

About that time he was a successful crochet lace designer and a supervisor for Dwyer & Co Limited in Cork, a progressive firm who had received a medal for their very well-worked and well-designed crochet in the 1883 Exhibition at Cork[3]. He studied at the Cork School of Art during the 1880s. He was a friend of Mlle Eleonore Riego de la Branchardière[4] and probably collaborated with her when she tried to improve and promote Irish crochet shortly before her death in the late 1880s as outlined in my other book[5]. He provided an affidavit to assist the legal process of setting up the Branchardière Trust Fund with money she left in her will to assist the Irish crochet and lace workers.

There are references to Michael Holland as a dealer or agent between 1904 and 1920 when he supplied many of the big shops in Cork. He was listed in the Irish Industrial Exhibition, World's Fair, St Louis, 1904[6], with 'coarse crochet d'oyleys, screens, bedspreads, shams, fringed borders, cushion covers, fine crochet lace collars, sets, insertions, edgings and coverlets. His street address was 12 Fitton St, Cork and his business was large enough to have the telegraphic address and code included in the World Fair Handbook.

Dwyer & Co were no longer listed as supplying crochet work or lace by 1919, although a business of the same name and the address was listed under bedding and hosiery in *Kenny's Irish Manufacturers Directory*[7].

Pat Earnshaw[8] wrote in her book on Youghal and other Irish laces that Michael Holland directed the production of some superb crochet pieces which secured awards at exhibitions in Dublin, Cork, Boston and London.

The written record with the Michael Holland Irish crochet lace collection in the Cork Museum notes:

> 'Lace made by Catherine Sheehan (and others) of hospital Lane (now 98th Street) who was the Grand-aunt of Mr. Noonan, 12 Brian Dillon Cresent [sic], Montenotte, Cork. Mr. Noonan remembers frequently taking crochet from Mrs. Sheehan's house to Mr. Michael Holland who was an agent and supplied many of the big shops in Cork City (c. 1915–1920).'

The later part of his long life (he lived to the age of 95, dying in 1950) was very different to his early time as a student at the Cork School of Art, employee of Dwyer & Co, the crochet dealer and protagonist of Alan Cole.

It appears that his financial situation improved at some stage, for his obituary presents him as a cultured gentleman of leisure, who contributed a pictorial feature 'This Quaint Old Cork of Ours' to the *Cork Weekly Examiner*. He was a member of the Cork Historical and Archaeological Society for 58 years. He was secretary and editor of the Journal of this Society in 1934–6, and president in 1942–6. He also wrote many articles for the Society's journal and for other local publications[9].

In his later years he often went tramping during weekends to places of historic or antiquarian interest and sketched them. Young people who were interested in the countryside and its relics were keen to join him, as he knew the local scene intimately and was good company. His obituary describes him as 'too reserved, too unassuming'; 'he was not one who went into the market place shouting his wares'. He was regarded with great affection by the Cork community. A daughter, Catherine Holland, was still alive at the time of his death[10].

Additional information is in the Michael Holland collection in the Cork City & County Archives.

Appendix VII

Crochet Lace Designers in the late 1800s.

A Designers Who Entered Crochet Lace in the Royal Dublin Society Competition in 1899[1].

Co. Cork

Miss Albina Collins, Camp Hill, Kinsale
Miss Margaret Crowley, Branch School of Art, Convent of Mercy, Kinsale
Miss Georgina MacKinlay, 13 Warren's Place, Cork.
Miss Mary T. Murphy, Branch School of Art, Convent of Mercy, Kinsale.
Miss Minnie Nagle, Ivy Cottage, Evergreen Rd, Cork.
Miss Marie Thullier, Branch School of Art, Convent of Mercy, Kinsale.
Miss Amy Whitelegge, Crawford School of Art, Cork.
Miss Emily Wilkinson, 31 Sydney Ave, Blackrock.

Co. Dublin

Miss Laura Clover, Blackrock.
Miss Louise Deane, Roseville, Donneykearney.
Miss Mary Doran, 28 James St, Dublin.
Miss Elizabeth Doyle, Rathmines Rd, Tourville
Miss Egan, 7 Sallymount Avenue, Leeson Park.
Miss Emily Scott, 15 Brighton Ave, Rathgar.
Miss Mary Tobias, 1 Eclipse Terrace, Belmont Avenue, Donnebrook *(sic.).*
Miss F. M. White, 63 Drumcondra Rd, Dublin.

Co. Limerick

Miss Agnes Buckley 2 Swanson Terrace, Limerick

B Women Who Won Awards for Crochet Design at the Cork School of Art

Caroline Beatson received the gold medal, the highest honour of the Department of Science and Art in London, the £25 Princess of Wales' Scholarship for her lace designs and a silver medal for crochet design in 1887. She was invited to London to attend lectures on designs and was one of the three students who spoke at James Brenan's farewell in 1889[2].

Albina Collins was one of a group of National Scholars from the Cork School to attend the South Kensington School of Art in the mid to late 1890s[3]. Later in life she was a teacher at the Central Technical School, Clonmel, Co. Tipperary[4]

**Georgina McKinlay* was another outstanding student at the Cork School where she had work accepted for the Art Mistresses' Certificate in 1893, won two prizes in 1896, including a bronze medal for a crochet design[5].

**Minnie Nagle* also had her work accepted for the Art Mistresses' Certificate in 1893 and received a bronze medal for lace designs at South Kensington[6].

Lizzie Perry was awarded two prizes in 1885 in London, probably for her crochet designs[7] and a silver medal for a set of crochet designs in 1895 in Cork[8].

**Amy Whitelegge* also qualified for her Art Mistresses' Certificate in 1893 and one of her designs illustrated James Brenan's article on the marketing of Irish lace in 1902 shown in Fig 7 14[9].

* indicates designers whose work appears in this book.

Appendix VIII

Collections of Irish Crochet Examined

Australia

Australian Lace Guild, NSW Branch, Sydney, NSW
Embroiderers Guild of NSW, Concord West, NSW
Embroiderers Guild of Western Australia, Perth, WA
Cavalcade of History and Fashion, Sydney, NSW
The Lace Place, Wave Rock, Hyden, WA
Powerhouse Museum, Ultimo, NSW
Personal collections of the author, Sybil Harland, Pat McGenniskin, Jeanette Moles and Phyll Morris

Republic of Ireland

Canal Stores, Clones, Co. Monaghan
Cork Municipal Museum, Cork, Co. Cork
Heritage and Lace Centre, Kenmare, Co. Kerry
Mary Aikenhead Heritage Centre, Harold's Cross, Dublin.
Monaghan Museum, Co. Monaghan
National Museum of Ireland, Collins Barracks, Dublin,
Public Museum, Kinsale, Co. Cork
Personal collections of Kathie Earle, Anne McCarthy, Nellie Ó Cléirigh, and Máire Treanor

Northern Ireland

Armagh County Museum, Armagh, Co. Armagh
Sheelin Lace Museum, Ballinaleck, Enniskillen, Co. Fermanagh
Ulster Folk and Transport Museum, Holywood, Co. Down

France

Personal Collection of Maryvonne Wetsch

United Kingdom

Victoria and Albert Museum, London

United States of America

Lacis Museum, Adeline St, Berkeley, California

The Irish Crochet on eBay (www.ebay.com) has been monitored almost continuously since November 2002.

Endnotes

Abbreviations
CCDB = Commissioner of Charitable Donations and Bequests, Dublin.
CC&CA = Cork City & County Archives
IIA= Irish Industries Association
MHC= Michael Holland Collection in CC&CA
PC = Power Correspondence in CC&CA

Introduction to Irish Crochet Technique
1 Recent Irish crochet pattern books such as those of Eithne d'Arcy, 1985 and Máire Treanor, 2002, refer to the ground between the motifs as the filling. However, I give many examples of the older Irish crochet which directly imitated the needle laces and include this interior mesh. For this reason, I have needed to use the term 'filling' in this book in the same way as employed for the needle laces. Thus the ground is between the motifs and the filling is within them.
2 Crocheted by Kathie Earle, who has won many prizes for her fine Irish crochet lace.

Chapter 1
1 Edwards & Williams, 1956; Bourke, 1993; Noone & Ronayne, 1996.
2 Hashagen & Levey, 2006.
3 Lindsey, 1886; Lindsey, & Biddle, 1883.
4 Newspaper article titled 'The Popularity of Crochet Work' of 4 May, 1889 in the MHC.
5 Lindsey & Biddle, 1883, p. 5; Boyle, 1971, p. 20.
6 Ballantyne, 2007.
7 Lindsey & Biddle, 1883, pp. 6–7.
8 Boyle, 1971, pp. 20–1.
9 Murphy, 1865.
10 Maguire, 1853, p. 204.
11 Maguire, 1853, p. 212.
12 Maguire, 1853, p. 205.
13 Maguire, 1853, p. 206.
14 Meredith, 1865, pp. 372–4; Lindsey & Biddle, 1883, pp. 6–7.
15 Maguire 1853, pp. 208–45.
16 Maguire pp. 215, 222, 226.
17 Maguire, 1853, p. 214.
18 Maguire, 1853, p. 221.
19 Maguire, 1853, p. 213.
20 Maguire, 1853, p. 223.
21 Maguire, 1853, pp. 2347; *Official Catalogue of the Great Industrial Exhibition*, 1853, p. 72; Cadogan & Falvey, 2006, p. 217.
22 Maguire, 1853, pp. 208, 223.
23 Lindsey & Biddle, 1883, p. 6.
24 www.ancestry.co.uk, 1851 census.
25 Meredith, 1865, p. 371.
26 Leslie, 2001, p. 1012; Dr. Susan Hood, Representative Church Body Library, Dublin, personal communication; www.ancestry.co.uk.
27 Meredith, 1865, p. 371.
28 Treanor, 2002.
29 Lindsey & Biddle, 1883, Lindsey, 1886, pp. 16–20.
30 *Official Catalogue of the Great Industrial Exhibition*, p. 70.
31 Meredith, 1865, pp. 19-23; Lindsey & Biddle, 1883, p. 7; Boyle, 1971, p. 54; Treanor, 2002, p. 17.
32 Meredith, 1865, p. 23.
33 Meredith, 1865, pp. 23, 371–2.
34 Boyle, 1971, p. 52.
35 Brenan, 1898, p. 84.
36 Blackburn, 1888, pp. 14, 17 quoted Lady Aberdeen's account of the Irish lace at the Edinburgh International Exhibition 1886.
37 Lindsey & Biddle, 1883, pp. 29–31; Meredith, 1865, pp. 46–9, 372–3; Boyle, 1971, p. 51.
38 Meredith, 1865, p. 44; Boyle, 1971, p. 51.
39 Boyle, 1971, p. xxii.
40 Lindsey & Biddle, 1883, p. 16.
41 Maguire, 1853, p 208–45; Meredith, 1865, pp. 40–1; Ó Cléirigh, 2003, pp. 91–106.
42 Meredith, 1865, pp. 2752, 374, Ó Cléirigh, 2003, p. 105.
43 Maguire, 1853, p. 208.
44 Maguire, 1853, pp. 209–11.
45 Meredith, 1865, pp. 221–223.
46 Meredith, 1865, p. 86.
47 Meredith, 1865, pp. 9–10, 90.
48 Ballantyne, 2007.
49 *Official Catalogue of the Great Industrial Exhibition*, 1852, 1853, p. 19.
50 Meredith, 1865, p. 216.
51 Brenan, 1902b, p. 429.
52 Longfield, 1978, Figs 34 and 35.
53 *Official Catalogue of the Great Industrial Exhibition 1852 1853*, p. 72; Lindsey & Biddle 1883, p. 16.
54 Meredith, 1865, p. 10.
55 Meredith, 1865, pp. 17, 37–8, 42.
56 Maguire, 1853, pp. 208–45.
57 Lindsey, 1886, p. 30; Levey, 1983, p. 94.
58 Palliser, 1865, p. 416; Lindsey, 1886, pp. 29–31; Meredith, 1865, pp. 2219, 240; Cole, 1890, p. 663.
59 O'Sullivan, 1991-2, p. 106.
60 Palliser, 1874, pp. 173–4.
61 Earnshaw, 1985, p. 95.
62 Boyle, 1971, p. 56.
63 Meredith, 1865, pp. 14–5; Lindsey, 1886, pp. 15–6.
64 Newspaper article titled 'The Popularity of Crochet Work' of 4 May, 1889 in the MHC.
65 Cork Industrial Exhibition 1883; 1886, p. 409. These comments were made by A. Connell, Juror for crochet and were quoted in the overall lace report made by A. Greaven, Upper Cross Mills, Kimmage, Dublin.
66 Newspaper article titled 'The Popularity of Crochet Work' of 4 May, 1889 in the MHC.

Chapter 2

1 Lindsey & Biddle, 1883; Lindsey, 1886; Levey, 1983; Frost, 1991; Toomer, 2001, pp. 11–2.

2 Lindsey & Biddle, 1883, p. 7.

3 This collar was identified as Irish crochet by Patricia Wardle in her book *Victorian Lace* of 1986, p. 36, Fig. 4.

4 Kauffmann, 1994, p. 45.

5 1983, Fig 440.

6 Berthas were in fashion in the period 1830–60, Toomer, 2001; pp. 168, 206.

An illustration of a fall cap with an estimated date of 1850-70 is shown in Toomer, 2001, pp. 74, 206.

A fall cap pattern of Marslands in 1953 is in the companion volume *Mademoiselle Riego and Irish Crochet Lace,* Ballantyne, 2007, p. 13.

A fanchon from 1847 is given in Fletcher, 1984, p. 91; Frost writes of fanchons being worn in the 1850s, 1991, p. 50 .

Cylindrical cuffs were shown in Fig 2.3 from the 1850s and were in the pattern book of Mlle Riego in 1856, *Crochet Book Fifteenth Series* and in Toomer, 2001, p. 88.

A bertha from the Victoria & Albert Museum featured in Ena Maidens *Technique of Irish Crochet* 1986, p. 103 has a particularly wide array of motifs. A fanchon in Caillard *et al.* (2003, p. 17) features different ones again. The d'oyleys shown by Eithne d'Arcy of Clones in *Irish Crochet Lace* (d'Arcy, 1984, pp. 1121) highlight other beautiful motifs.

7 Hardouin, [n.d.]b.

8 Lindsey & Biddle, 1883, p. 7.

9 Blackburn, 1888, pp. 14, 17; Mrs Palliser, 1874, pp. 173–74 believed it was made in 1851; Mrs. Hand entered Guipure in the 1853 Dublin Exhibition Official Catalogue of the Great Industrial Exhibition 1853, p. 70.

10 Palliser, 1874, p. 173–4; Lindsey, 1886, p.18; *Weldon's Practical Crochet* No 186 p. 9 [c.1901]; Boyle, 1971, p. 60.

11 Stillwell, 1996, p. 109; Toomer 2002, p. 46.

12 Lindsey & Biddle, 1883, p. 7.

13 This ground is very different to the ones in the standard pattern books DMC, c.1908, pp. 2833; *Mary Card's Irish Crochet Book No 3,* 1916; pp. 13–5; Maidens, 1986, pp. 6776 .

14 Hardouin, [n.d.]a; Card, 1913a, pp. 216, 227, Card, 1917, pp. 65–8.

15 Paludan, 1995, p. 64 shows a fall cap and Maidens, 1986, p. 146 includes a fichu, both of which are in the collection of the Victoria & Albert Museum.

Another fall cap is in the Sheelin Lace Museum, Bellanaleck, Enniskillen, Co. Fermanagh, Northern Ireland. (Cathcart, 1999, and at www.irishlacemuseum.com).

A fanchon was part of the Irish crochet exhibition of Lacis, Berkeley, California, April 30 to July 30, 2005, www. lacismuseum.com.

The handkerchief in Gwynne, 1997, p. 66 is a fine example of this style

As indicated earlier, these accessories were fashionable in the 1850s.

16 Lindsey & Biddle, 1883.

17 Lindsey & Biddle, 1883.

18 Hardouin, [n.d.]a; Card, 1913b, pp. 332–3; Card, 1916, pp. 68–72).

19 The Ulster Folk and Transport Museum, Cultra, Northern Ireland has two collars, numbers 1972/143 and 1972/26 both in shapes typical of the 1850s and with similar motifs, meandering stems and background of 'stars' with many spokes. The latter collar has relatively bold alternating motifs forming the outer edge. The same overall and edge motifs were used for a flounce from Clones in the National Museum of Ireland Number 1981/3.

20 The museum records describe it as a 'collar à la chevalière', suggesting that it was part of a riding habit (Clare Browne, Victoria & Albert Museum, personal communication).

21 Pullan, 1859, p. 53.

22 Hardouin, [n.d.]b.

23 Inscription on the display; Blake, 2001.

24 d'Arcy, 1985, pp.11–21; Treanor, 2002.

Chapter 3

1 Lindsey & Biddle, 1883; Lindsey, 1886.

2 Palliser, 1865, p. 416.

3 Stillwell, 1996, p. 129.

4 Lindsey & Biddle, 1883, p. 7; Lindsey, 1886, pp. 18–9.

5 Lindsey, & Biddle, 1883, p. 7.

6 Lindsey & Biddle, 1886, pp. 7–8.

7 Lovesey & Barley, 1986, pp. 8–10; Toomer, 2001, pp. 42–9.

8 Lindsey & Biddle, 1883, p. 7.

9 Lindsey, 1886, p. 18.

10 Maguire, 1853, p. 211; Meredith, 1865, pp. 42–45, 73–74, 95.

11 Mrs Meredith, 1965, p. 8 wrote that 'sewed' muslin was an 'old acquaintance' in Ireland.

12 Riego, 1849.

13 Calavas, A [n.d.] Fig 2.3, Flower, 1984, pp. 80–1; Ballantyne, 2007, pp .

14 Hardouin, [n.d.]b.

15 Maguire, 1853; Meredith 1865; Lindsey & Biddle, 1883; Lindsey 1886, quoted by Ballantyne 2007

Chapter 4

1 Ballantyne, 2007.

2 Le Bouquet de Fleurs Collar in Riego, 1848 and Crochet Collar –British Emblems in Riego, 1849.

3 Riego 1849.

4 Maguire, 1853, pp. 208-9.

5 Riego, 1853.

6 Riego, 1853, *The Needle*, Vol II, No 14.

7 Card, 1916, p 49.

8 Meredith, p. 241.

9 Hardouin, [n.d.]b.

10 Riego, 1853.

11 Letter beginning 'this settled but it will be a tax on my time', in the Power correspondence, Cork City & County Archives.

12 Ballantyne, 2007.

13 Levey, 1983, Fig. 172. V & A No 1504–1900 .

14 Mme Ashton [c.1849]

15 Potter 1855b, p. 112. lists a *German Raised Crochet Book*, written by J. C. E. A., but I was unable to find a copy.

16 Boutellier, 1873; Caulfeild & Saward, 1882, p. 114.

Chapter 5

1 O'Flannagan & Buttimer, 1993, pp. 813–72.
2 Michael Holland Collection in the Cork County & City Archives.
3 Cole, 1890, pp. 661–2.
4 Brenan, 1898, p. 77.
5 Cork Industrial Exhibition 1883, 1886, pp. 2745; Brenan, 1898, pp. 76–7.
6 Brenan, 1898, p. 78.
7 Cole, 1885; 1889; 1898.
8 Cole, 1888; Bonython, & Burton, 2003, p. 280.
9 Brenan, 1898, p. 78.
10 Cole, 1885, pp. 1–2; Lindsey, 1886, p. 31; Cole, 1890, p. 665; Brenan, 1898, pp. 101–2.
11 Mulligan, 1902, p. 152.
12 Murray, 1993, pp. 856–7.
13 Murray, 1993, p. 859, quoting from the *Cork Examiner* 16 April, 1885.
14 Murray, 1993, p. 862.
15 Brenan, 1898, p. 78.
16 www.crawfordartgallery.com/1876–1900.html, p. 12.
17 Cole, 1889, p. 4.
18 Murray, 1993, p. 863.
19 www.crawfordartgallery.com/1876-1900. html, p. 22.
20 Turpin, 1995, p. 179.
21 Brenan, 1902a, p. 147; Turpin, 1995, p. 179.
22 Boyle 1971, pp. 104, 108, 111; Turpin, 1995, pp. 170, 179, 181.
23 Turpin, 1995, p. 181.
24 Brenan, 1902b, p. 429; Boyle, 1971, p. 42.
25 Turpin, 1995, p. 181.
26 Boyle, 1971, p. 139.
27 Turpin, 1995, pp 161, 163, 167–9, 178, 182–4.
28 The original of the newspaper correspondence in which this claim was made (*Irish Textile Journal,* 29 July 1890) was not seen, but the reply is in the later issue of 15 October 1890 which is in the MHC.
29 *Irish Textile Journal,* 15 October, 1890, in the MHC.
30 *Irish Textile Journal,* 18 November, 1890 in the MHC.
31 Irish Lacemaking, Letter to the Editor of the *Freeman,* March 15, 1891.
32 United States Consulate Cork, Cork Examiner, 4 May 1889, in the MHC.
33 Lindsey & Biddle, 1883; Lindsey, 1886.
34 Boyle, 1971, pp. 48, 93.
35 Murray, 1993, pp. 856-7; www.whytes.ie./Biographies/BiogsAE.htm#brenan.

Chapter 6

1 Coyne, 1902; Turpin, 1995; Cole, 1897; Boyle, 1971, pp. 38–142; Treanor, 2002, pp. 1924; Ó Cléirigh, 2003, pp. 91–106, 147–67.
2 Death Certificate.
3 Ó Cléirigh, 1985, p. 17; 2003, p. 99; Earnshaw 1888a, p. 2; 1993, p. 8.
4 Lindsey, 1886; Lindsey & Biddle, 1883.
5 Turpin, 1995, pp. 193, 201; Ó Cléirigh, 2003, pp. 147–167.
6 Boyle, 1971, p. 93.
7 Boyle, 1971, pp. 948.
8 World's Columbian Exhibition, Guide to the Irish Industrial Village, 1893, 92011-3, No 3, p. 1; Brenan, 1898, p. 101; Ó Cléirigh, 1985, pp 16–7; 2003, pp. 154–6.
9 Treanor, 2002, pp. 1920.
10 Ó Cléirigh, 1985, p. 17.
11 Martin, R.M., 1907; map opposite p. 258 in The Congested Districts Board for Ireland, 1902, pp. 258–270; Boyle 1971, p. 60
12 Science Teaching and Technical Instruction, 1902, pp. 173–4; Boyle, 1971, pp. xxii, 60; Treanor, 2002, p. 24.
13 Boyle, 1971, p. 57; Ó Cléirigh, 2003, p. 105.
14 Boyle, 1971, p. 62.
15 Boyle, 1971, pp. 132–6.
16 Mairead Dunleavy, former textile curator at the National Museum of Ireland, quoted by Treanor, 2002, p. 24.
17 Science Teaching and Technical Instruction, 1902, p. 173.
18 Science Teaching and Technical Instruction, 1902, p. 173.
19 Ó Cléirigh, 2003, pp. 104–5.
20 Boyle, 1971, p. 55.
21 Boyle, 1971, p. 62.
22 Cole, 1897, p. 10.
23 Cole, 1897, p. 8.
24 Treanor, 2002, p. 25.
25 Treanor, 2002, pp. 23–4.
26 Article of Isabel Madden in the local Fermanagh newspaper, *Impartial Reporter* c.1898 quoted in Treanor 2003, pp. 19–20.
27 Cole, 1897, p. 11.
28 *Needlework Practical Journal,* No 21, c. 1900.
29 Cole 1890, p. 664; Madden c. 1898 quoted by Treanor, 2002, pp. 1920.
30 Treanor, 2002, pp. 19–20.
31 Brenan, 1898, p. 102; Isabel Madden c.1898 in Treanor 2002, p. 20.
32 Royal Dublin Society 1902, pp. 80; Boyle, 1971, pp. xxiii, 11–2; Turpin 1995, p. 131.
33 RDS National Crafts Competition Winners Exhibition 2005.
34 Trainor 2002, pp. 21–2.
35 Kenny, 1919.
36 Boyle, 1971, pp. 8895; Treanor, 2002, pp. 25–9.
37 Cole, 1890, p. 664.
38 Cole, 1897, p. 6.
39 Cole, 1889, p. 5.

Chapter 7

1 www.crawfordartgallery.com.1876-1900.html, pp. 14–5, accessed 11 May 2006
2 Cole, 1888.
3 Cole, 1889, p. 4.
4 Lefébure, 1899, p. 253.
5 Cork Museum records with the Michael Holland Irish Crochet Collection.
6 Turnbull, 1904, Vol I, p. 6.
7 The details of this group of laces are from the records of the Cork Museum.
8 Cole, 1888, Section 5.
9 Boutellier, 1873; Caulfeild & Saward, 1882, p. 110; *Mrs.*

Leach's Fancy Work Basket, March 1886, Vol I No 6, p 112, No 8, p. 153.
10 Cole 1888, Section 5 shows a matching pair of Reticella border and insertion and a grape border which has the matching insertion in Maidens pp. 80–1.
11 Riego, 1887.
12 *Weldon's Practical Crochet* No 188
13 www.crawfordartgallery.com.1876–1900.html
14 Walters & Cosh, 1986, pp. 13-4.
15 Brenan 1902c, opposite pp. 432, 435.
16 Cole, 1902, Plates 28-30.
17 Maidens 1986 This is Number 1914 199 in the National Museum of Ireland. This is part of a set in this style which included another collar 1914 200 and table centre 1914 201.
18 National Museum of Ireland, Cork Public Museum; Potter, 1990, pp. 116–7.
19 Brenan, 1902b, p. 429.
20 Boyle, 1971, p. 55.
21 Cole, 1885, pp. 2–4.
22 James Brenan, 1902b, opp p. 431. Others may be found in Alan Cole 1902, Pl 28; Maidens, 1986, p. 97; Paludan, 1986, p. 61 and Levey, 1983, Pl. 481.
23 Cole, 1889, p. 5.
24 Cole, 1897, p. 2.
25 Turpin, 1995, p. 179.
26 *Scrapbook of the Royal Dublin Society Lace Competition for 1899,* 1899.
27 Brenan, 1902a, opp. p. 147; Boyle 1971, pp. 104, 108, 111; Turpin, 1995; p. 170.
28 Cole, 1897 p. 10, Isabel Madden in the *Impartial Reporter* c. 1898 quoted by Treanor, 2002, p. 20.
29 Treanor, 2002, p. 24.
30 d'Arcy, 1985.
31 Treanor, 2002.
32 Brenan, 1902b, p. 429.
33 *The Story of Clones Lace*, Brochure from Monaghan, the Lace County of Ireland, n.d. obtained 2005.
34 Treanor, 2002, pp. 10, 33, 36, 95.
35 Cole, 1890, p. 664.
36 Science Teaching and Technical Instruction, 1902, p. 173.
37 Ballantyne, 2007.

Appendix I
1 Franklin, 2005.
2 Cadogan & Falvey, 2006, p. 194; Catalogue of the National Library of Ireland, www.nli.ie.
3 Maguire, 1853, p. 222.
4 Cadogan & Falvey, 2006, p. 200; Catalogue of the British Library, www.bl.uk.
5 www.ancestry.co.uk, 1851 and 1861 censuses.
6 Meredith 1865, p. 23; Lindsey, 1883, p. 16.
7 Treanor, 2002, p. 9.
8 Burtchaell & Sadleir, 1924, p. 707.
9 Leslie, 2001, p. 1012 and Dr. Susan Hood, Representative Church Body Library, Dublin, personal communication.
10 Meredith, 1865, p. 371.
11 Lindsey & Biddle, 1883.

Appendix II
1 *Official Catalogue of the Great Industrial Exhibition, 1853.*

Appendix III
1 Bonython & Burton, 2003, p. 280.
2 Bonython & Burton, 2003.
3 *The Honiton Lace Industry in 1887*; Levey, 1983, p. 114.
4 Cole, 1892.
5 Hashagen & Levey, 2006, p. 8.
6 www.vam.ac.uk, and Whiting, 1920, pp. 267–9.
7 *Encyclopaedia Britannica* pp. 37–42 + five pages of illustrations.
8 Turpin 1995, p. 169.
9 Murray, 1993, p. 849; Turpin, 1995, pp. 169, 182, 189. www.whytes.ie./Biographies/BiogsAE.htm#brenan.
10 Brenan, 1887; Turpin, 1995, p. 182; Murray, 1993, p. 863; www.crawfordartgallery.com/1876-1900, p. 14; www.whytes.ie./Biographies/BiogsAE.htm#brenan, .
11 Holland, 1943, p. 101; www.whytes.ie./Biographies/BiogsAE.htm#brenan.
12 www.crawfordartgallery.com/1876–1900, p. 6.
13 Turpin, 1995, pp. 161–85.

Appendix IV
1 Boyle, 1971, pp. 132v5.

Appendix V
1 Cole, 1897, p. 9; Boyle, 1971, p. 57; Treanor, 2002, p. 22.
2 Treanor, 2002, pp. 21–22.

Appendix VI
1 C.Ó.S, 1950, p. 126v7; Cadogan & Falvey, 2006, p. 137.
2 Irish Artisans Exhibition, 1885, p. 45.
3 Cork Industrial Exhibition 1883, 1886, pp. 408–9.
4 Turnbull, 1904, Vol I, p. 6.
5 Ballantyne, 2007.
6 *Handbook and Catalogue of Exhibitors*, 1904, p. 163.
7 Kenny, 1919.
8 Earnshaw, 1988a, p. 31.
9 C.Ó.S, 1950, pp. 126–7; Cadogan & Falvey, 2006, p. 137.
10 C.Ó.S, 1950, pp. 126–7.

Appendix VII
1 *Scrapbook of the Royal Dublin Society Lace Competition for 1899,* 1899.
2 www.crawfordartgallery.com/1876–1900.html, pp. 12, 14.
3 Mulligan, 1902, p. 153-4; www.crawfordartgallery.com/1876–1900.html, p.20
4 Boyle, 1971, p. 79.
5 Mulligan, 1902, pp. 153–4; www.crawfordartgallery.com/1876–1900.html, p. 1920.
6 www.crawfordartgallery.com/1876–1900.html, pp. 17, 20.
7 Cole 1885, pp. 2–3.
8 www.crawfordartgallery.com/1876–1900.html, p. 19.
9 Brenan, 1902a, p. 435; www.crawfordartgallery.com/1876–1900.html, p. 17.

References and Bibliography

Auerbach, Jeffrey A., c.1999, *Great Exhibition of 1851: a Nation on Display*, Yale University Press, New Haven, Connecticut.

Ballantyne, Barbara, 2002, *Mary Card: Australian Crochet Lace Designer*, Ballantyne, Sydney.

— 2007, *Mademoiselle Riego and Irish Crochet Lace*, Ballantyne, Sydney.

Ballard, Linda, 1992, Irish Lace: Tradition or Commodity? *Journal of Ethological Studies and Folk Life* 31:43-56.

Blackburn, Helen, (editor), 1888, *Handy Book of Reference for Irish Women*, Irish Exhibition in London.

Blake, Donal S., 2001, *Mary Aikenhead (1787–1858) Servant of the Poor*, Caritas, Dublin

Bonython, Elizabeth & Burton, Anthony, 2003, *The Great Exhibitor: the Life and Work of Henry Cole*, V & A Publications, London.

Bourke, Austin, 1993, *The Visitation of God? The Potato and the Great Irish Famine*, Lilliput Press, Dublin.

Boutillier, E. & J., [1873], *'Eugenie' Crochet Book for Antimacassars*, Simpkin Marshall, London.

Boyle, Elizabeth, 1971, *The Irish Flowerers*, Ulster Folk Museum, County Down & Institute of Irish Studies, Belfast.

Breathnach, Clara, 2005, *The Congested Districts Board of Ireland: Poverty and Development in the West of Ireland, 1891–1923*, Four Courts Press, Dublin.

Brenan, James, 1887. *Report on a visit to Paris and Belgium Respecting the Manufacture of Needlepoint Lace*. School of Art, Cork. Listed by Whiting, 1920, p. 259.

— 1898, 'The Modern Irish Lace Industry', *Arts and Crafts Society of Ireland Journal*, 1, pp. 69–103.

— 1902a, Art Instruction in Ireland - Metropolitan School of Art, Dublin, pp. 146–8, Coyne, W.P., (editor), *Ireland Industrial and Agricultural*, Browne & Nolan, Dublin.

— 1902b, The Modern Irish Lace Industry, pp. 420–432, Coyne, W.P., (editor), *Ireland Industrial and Agricultural*, Browne & Nolan, Dublin.

— 1902c, The Marketing of Irish Lace, pp .433–5, Coyne, W.P., (editor), *Ireland Industrial and Agricultural*, Browne & Nolan, Dublin.

Brown, Alan, 2002, *Lace and the Emerald Isle*, Brown, Sawbridgeworth, Herts, England

Buckley, J. J., 1913, *Irish Lace*, Museum Bulletin, National Museum of Science and Art, Vol III, Part 1, Dublin.

Burtchaell, George Dames & Sadleir, Thomas Ulick, 1924, *Alumni Dublinenses: A Register of the Students, Graduates, Professors, and Provosts of Trinity College, in the University of Dublin*, London, Williams & Norgate.

Cadogan, Tim & Falvey, Jeremiah, 2006, *A Biographical Dictionary of Cork*, Four Courts, Dublin.

Caillard, France, Cosquer, Aline, Guichaoua, Rosa, Le Berre, Gwenaël, Madec, Yohan, Tanter, Fredéréric & Wetsch-Cloarec, Maryvonne, 2003, *De la Crise de la Sardine à l'âge d'or de la Dentelle*, Éditions Ouest-France, Rennes.

Calavas, A (éditeur), [n.d.] *Collection A. Lescure: Cols en Broderies et en Dentelles milieu du Dix Neuvième Siécle*, Paris, Libraire des Arts Décoratifs.

Card, Mary, 1913a, 'How to Make Real Old Irish Lace: Beginning a New Series of Lessons', *Everylady's Journal*, April, 1913, pp. 216, 227.

— 1913b, 'How to Make Real Old Irish Lace: Second of a New Series of Lessons', *Everylady's Journal*, June, 1913, pp.332–3.

— 1916, *Mary Card's Crochet Book No 3, Irish Crochet*, Fitchett Brothers, Melbourne.

Carter. W., [c. 1851], *Royal Exhibition Knitting, Netting and Crochet Book*, J. T. Wood, London

Cathcart, Rosemary, 1999, *The Sheelin Antique Irish Lace Collection*, Cathcart, Bellanaleck, Enniskillen, Co Fermanagh, Northern Ireland.

Caulfeild, S. F. A. & Saward, Blanche C., 1882, *Dictionary of Needlework*, Upcott Gill, London.

Cole, Alan S., 1884, *Two Lectures on the Art of Lacemaking*, Metropolitan School of Art, Dublin, February, 1884.

— 1885, *Report Upon Visits to Convents, Classes and Schools where Lace-making and Designing for Lace are taught, as well as upon the Steps Taken for Assisting the Development of the Lace Industry in Ireland.*

— 1888, *A Renascence of the Irish Art of Lace-making*, Chapman & Hall, London.

— 1889, *Irish lace: Report by Mr. Alan S. Cole on His Visits to Lace-making Centres*, April 1889,

— 1890, 'Lacemaking in Ireland', *English Illustrated Magazine*, June: pp. 655–68.

— 1892, *Report on Northampton, Bucks, and Beds Lacemaking, November 1891*, London.

— 1897, *Report by Mr. Alan Cole upon his Visits to Irish Lacemaking and Embroidery Schools in 1897, Department of Science and Art.*

— 1902, *Irish Lace*, Howitt & Son, Nottingham. The thirty large plates bear the imprint of Julius Hoffmann, a Stuttgart publisher.

Congested Districts Board for Ireland, 1902, pp. 258–70, Coyne, W.P., (editor), 1902, *Ireland Industrial and Agricultural*, Browne & Nolan, Dublin.

Cork Industrial Exhibition 1883; 1886, *Report of Executive Committee, Award of Jurors and Statements of Accounts*, Purcell, Cork

Coyne, W.P., (editor), *Ireland Industrial and Agricultural*, Browne & Nolan, Dublin.

C.Ó.S, 1950, 'Obituary: The late Mr. Michael Holland', *Journal of the Cork Historical and Archaeological Society*, 55, pp. 126–7.

de Dillmont, Therese, [c.1886] *Encyclopaedia of Needlework*, DMC Mulhause. This classic book, first published in French was later translated into English, German and other languages. The contents changed over the years without any indication of date or edition. The copy referred to in this book had the same crochet as one inscribed with the date 1888 at Kenmare.

Department of Agriculture and Technical Instruction pp. 271–94, Coyne, W.P., (editor), *Ireland Industrial and Agricultural,* Browne & Nolan, Dublin.

D'Arcy, Eithne, 1984, *Irish Crochet Lace*, Dolmen Press, Mountrath, Ireland.

DMC, [undated c. 1908], *La Guipure d'Irlande,* Dolfus, Mieg et Cie, Mulhausen, Alsace. Translated into English (*Irish Crochet Lace*), Italian and German. Even though Therese de Dillmont is given as editor, there are reports of her death many years earlier. For example, Maryvonne Wetsch-Cloarec, p. 63 in Caillard *et al.* 2003 reported that she died on 22 May 1890 at Baden-Baden and that her niece Alice Morawska continued her work. The English magazine *Queen* of 15 February 1908, p. 300 mentions that "a French book on Irish crochet lace is also included in the Therese Dillmont Series on Art Needlework".

DMC, [undated], *Needle-made Laces, First Series*, DMC Library, Mulhause.

Earnshaw, Pat, 1980, *The Identification of Lace*, Shire, Princes Risborough, Aylesbury, Bucks, UK.

— 1982, *A Dictionary of Lace*, Shire, Princes Risborough, Aylesbury, Bucks, UK,

— 1985, *Lace in Fashion from the Sixteenth to the Twentieth Centuries*, Batsford, London.

— 1988a, *Youghal and Other Irish Laces*, Gorse, Surrey, England.

— 1988b, *Embroidered Machine Nets: Limerick and Worldwide*, Gorse, Surrey, England.

Edwards, R. Dudley & Williams, T. Desmond, 1956, (editors), *The Great Famine: Studies in Irish History, 1845-52*, Published for the Irish Committee of Historical Sciences by Browne & Nolan, Dublin.

Elise, Mme, (editor), No 3 Irish Jesuit Crochet Lace, and How to Work it, pp. 28 In *Bow Bells Art Work Instructor, Supplement Published with Bow Bells*, December 1883.

Exhibition of the Works of Industry of All Nations, 1851; Reports by the Juries on the Subjects in the 30 Classes into which the Exhibition was Divided, 1852, p. 409, Spicer Brothers, London

Fletcher, Marion, 1966, *Female Costume in the Nineteenth Century*, Oxford University Press, Melbourne.

Fletcher, Marion, 1984, *Costume in Australia 1788–1901*, Oxford University Press, Melbourne.

Flower, Cedric, 1984, *Clothes in Australia: A Pictorial History 17881980s*, Kangaroo Press, Sydney.

Franklin, Margaret, 2005, *A Bibliography of Limerick City and County*, Doon South Press, Limerick.

Frost, Lenore, 1991, *Dating Family Photos 1850–1920*, Frost, Melbourne.

Gorges, Mary, 1899, Irish Home Industries: Carrickmacross and Limerick Lace and Clare Embroidery, *Chambers Journal,* Part 18, June 1 1899, p. 375–8.

Goubaud, Mme Adolphe [Marie], 1869, *Madame Goubaud's Crochet Book*, Ward, Lock & Tyler, London.

Gwynne, Judyth L., 1997, *The Illustrated Dictionary of Lace*, Batsford, London.

Hall, Mr. & Mrs. S.C. 18-- , *Ireland; its Scenery, Character, &c.*, Hall, Virtue & Co, London.

Hardouin, G., [n.d.]a, *Album de Dentelle d'Irlande Fine, Cinquième Volume*, Cotons L.V. et M.F.A., [Paris].

— [n.d.]b, *Album de Dentelle d'Irlande Ancienne, Sixième Volume*, Cotons L.V. et M.F.A. [Paris].

Hashagen, Joanna & Levey, Santina, 2006, *Fine and Fashionable: Lace from the Blackborne Collection*, Bowes Museum, Barnard Castle, County Durham.

Holland, Michael, 1894, Irish Laces, *Journal of the Cork Historical and Archaeological Society*, IIIA, 197–8.

— 1943, Cork City; Its History and Antiquities, *Journal of the Cork Historical and Archaeological Society,* XLVIII, No 167, pp. 99–105.

Hughes, Kathryn, 2005, *The Short Life and Long Times of Mrs. Beeton*, Fourth Estate, London.

Illustrated Exhibitor, Tribute to the World's Industrial Jubilee Comprising Sketches By Pen and Pencil of Principal Objects in the Great Exhibition of the Industry of All Nations, 1851, Cassell, London, p. 331.

Kauffmann, C. M., 1994, *Old Paintings Survey 1994, Victoria & Albert Museum Catalogue of Foreign Paintings II. 1800–1900*, Victoria & Albert Museum, London.

Kenny, Kevin J., 1919, *Kenny's Irish Manufacturers Directory:* 1919, Archive CD Books, Dublin.

Konior, Mary, 1987, *Heritage Crochet: An Analysis*, Dryad Press, London.

Kurella, Elizabeth, 1998, *Guide to Lace and Linens*, Antique Trader Books, Dubuque, Iowa.

Lansdell, Avril, 1985, *Fashion à la Carte 1860 –1900; A Study of Fashion through Cartes-de-visite*, History in Camera Series, Shire, Princes Risborough, Aylesbury, Bucks, UK.

Lefébure, Ernest, 1899, *Embroidery and Lace: Their Manufacture and History*, Translated and enlarged with notes by A.S.C. [Alan S. Cole], H. Grevel, London.

Leslie, Canon J.B., (compiler), 2001, *Clergy of Dublin and Glendalough; Biographical Succession Lists,* 2001, revised, edited and updated by W.J. R. Wallace, Diocese of Dublin and Glendalough, Dublin.

Levey, Santina M., 1983, *Lace: A History*, Victoria & Albert Museum, London.

Lindsey, Ben & Biddle, C. Harry (compilers), 1883, *Mansion House Exhibition: Irish Lace, A History of the Industry with Illustrations.* Under the Patronage of the Queen and the Prince and Princess of Wales.

— 1886, *Irish Lace: its Origins and History*, Hodges, Figgis & Co, Dublin

Longfield, Ada, 1978, *Irish Lace*, Irish Heritage Series 21, Eason, Dublin.

— 1982, *Guide to the Collection of Lace*, National Museum of Ireland, Dublin.

Lovesey, Nenia & Barley, Catherine, 1986, *Venetian Gros Point Lace*, Dryad, London.

McGinnity, Annie, 1992, A History of Crochet in the Roslea/Clones/Aghadrumsee Area, *Roslea Community Historical Society Journal* 1, 15–9.

Maguire, J.F. 1853, *The Industrial Movement in Ireland as Illustrated by the National Exhibition of 1852,* O'Brien, Cork.

Maidens, Ena, 1986, *The Technique of Irish Crochet Lace*, Batsford, London.

Marslands Manual of New and Original Registered Designs in Crochet, Guipure, Lacet and Embroidery, 1853, Marslands, Manchester.

Martin, R.M., 1907, The Manufacture of Lace and Crochet in Ireland, pp. 12843 W.T. M.-F [W.T. Macartney-Filgate], (editor), 1907, *Irish Rural Life and Industry*, Irish International Exhibition 1907, Home Industries Section, Hely's, Dublin.

Meredith, Mrs [Susanna], 1865, *The Lacemakers: Sketches of Irish Character*, Jackson, Walford & Hodder, London.

Mulligan, W., 1902, Art Instruction in Ireland –The Crawford Municipal School of Art, Cork, pp. 152–4, Coyne, W.P., (editor), *Ireland Industrial and Agricultural*, Browne & Nolan, Dublin.

Murphy, Reverend Dominick, 1865, *Sketches of Irish Nunneries,* James Duffy, Dublin.

Murray, Peter, 1993, Art Institutions in Nineteenth-century Cork, pp. 813872 *Cork History and Society: Interdisciplinary Essays on the History of an Irish County*, edited by O'Flannagan, Patrick & Buttimer, Cornelius G., Geography Publications, Dublin.

Noone, Val & Ronayne, Jarlath, (editors), 1996, Introduction p. ix, the Australian Commemoration of the Great Irish Famine, Proceedings of Conferences March 1996, Victoria University, Melbourne.

Official Catalogue of the Great Industrial Exhibition (in Connection with the Royal Dublin Society), *1853*, Falconer, Dublin.

Ó Cléirigh, Nellie, 1985, *Carrickmacross Lace: Irish Embroidered Net Lace*, Colin Smythe, Buckinghamshire.

—2003, *Hardship and High Living: Irish Women's Lives 1808–1923*, Portobello Press, Dublin.

—& Rowe, Veronica, 1995, *Limerick Lace: a Social History and a Maker's Manual,* Colin Smythe, Gerrards Cross.

O'Sullivan, Patrick V., 1991-2, 'Kenmare Lace', pp. 106–8, *Irish Arts Review*.

Palliser, Mrs Bury, 1865, *The History of Lace*, Samson, Low, Son & Marston, London.

—, 1874, The International Exhibition 1874, *Art Journal*, pp. 173–4.

Paludan, Lis, 1995, *Crochet: History and Technique,* Interweave, Loveland, Colorado, USA.

Potter, Annie Louise, 1990, *A Living Mystery: The International Art & History of Crochet*, A.J. Publishing, USA.

Potter, Esther, 1955a, English Knitting and Crochet Books of the Nineteenth Century, *Transactions of the Bibliographical Society* 10: 25–40.

— 1955b, English Knitting and Crochet Books of the Nineteenth Century, *Transactions of the Bibliographical Society* 10: 10319.

Pullan, Mrs [Matilda Marian], 1859, *The Ladies' Manual of Fancy-work*, Dick & Fitzgerald, New York.

Quinlan, Sr. M. Patricia, [undated c. 2000], *Lacemaking in Kinsale,* pp. 65–67 from unknown book.

Reid, Richard, 1996, The Great Famine – Australian Connections, pp. 21–30 *The Australian Commemoration of the Great Irish Famine, Proceedings of Conferences*, March 1996, Victoria University, Melbourne.

Riego de la Branchardière, Mlle Eleonore, 1848, *Crochet Book, Fourth Series*, Simpkin Marshall, London.

— 1848, *Crochet Book, Fourth Series*, Simpkin Marshall, London.

— 1849, *Crochet Book, Fifth Series*, Simpkin Marshall, London.

— 1853, *Crochet Book, Thirteenth Series,* Simpkin Marshall, London.

Royal Dublin Society, 1902, pp 17580, Coyne, W.P., (editor), *Ireland Industrial and Agricultural,* Browne & Nolan, Dublin.

Science Teaching and Technical *Instruction* 1902a, pp. 155–74 Coyne, W.P., (editor), *Ireland Industrial and Agricultural,* Browne & Nolan, Dublin.

Scrapbook of the Royal Dublin Society Lace Competition for 1899, 1899, Royal Dublin Society, Dublin.

Stillwell, Alexandra, 1996, *Illustrated Dictionary of Lacemaking*, Cassel, London.

The Story of Clones Lace, Brochure from Monaghan, the Lace County of Ireland, n.d. obtained 2005

Todd, Pat & Deddis, Pat (editors), 2004, *Lace and Lacemaking in Ireland*, Members of the Lace Guild of Northern Ireland in Conjunction with Ulster Folk & Transport Museum.

Toomer, Heather, 2001, *Antique Lace: Identifying Types and Techniques*, Schiffer, Atglen, Pennsylvania.

— 2002, *European Laces–an Introduction*, Toomer, UK.

Treanor, Máire, 2002, *Clones Lace: The Story and Patterns of an Irish Crochet*, Mercier, Cork.

Turnbull, Mrs Rivers, (editor), 1904–1905, *The Selected Works of Mlle Riego (Mlle Riego de la Branchardière), the Eminent Writer on Crochet, Knitting, Lacework , &c.,* Vols I–IV, Horace Cox, London.

Turner, Pauline, 1984, *Crochet: A History of the Craft since 1850*, Shire, Princes Risborough, Aylesbury, Bucks, UK.

Turpin, John, W., 1995, *A School of Art in Dublin Since the Eighteenth Century: A History of the National College of Art and Design*, Gill & McMillan, Dublin.

Walters, James & Cosh, Sylvia, (compilers), 1986, *The Harmony Guide to Crochet Stitches, Volume I*, Lyric, London.

Walters, Johanna O'Mahony, 2001, *Merci Beaucoup: A Story of Courage and Compassion, Convent of Mercy, Kinsale, 1844–2002*, Bandon.

Wardle, Patricia, 1986, *Victorian Lace*, Herbert Jenkins, London.

Warren, Mrs [Eliza] & Pullan, Mrs [Matilda Marian], 1855, *Treasures of Needlework*, Ward Lock, London, Facsimile edition, Lancer Books, New York, 1973. (The first names come from the British Library catalogue)

Weldon's Practical Crochet 1886–1910.

www.ancestry.co.uk

www.catalogue.bl.uk

www.crawfordartgallery.com/

www.ebay.com

www.irishlacemuseum.com

www.lacismuseum.org/irish_crochet.html

www.marlamallett.com/1-124ds.htm

www.vam.ac.uk/nationalartlibrary

www.whytes.ie./Biographies/BiogsAE.htm#brenan

Index